Talk, Talk, Sweet Charlotte

Dean A. Le' Breton

authorHOUSE®

AuthorHouse™
1663 Liberty Drive
Bloomington, IN 47403
www.authorhouse.com
Phone: 1-800-839-8640

First published by AuthorHouse   5/8/2009

ISBN: 978-1-4389-7271-8 (sc)
ISBN: 978-1-4389-7272-5 (hc)

Printed in the United States of America
Bloomington, Indiana

This book is printed on acid-free paper.

CHAPTER 1

"DEAN, YOU ARE TO REPORT to the junior high school immediately." These words would redirect the focus of my job and ultimately change my life. The principal of an elementary school in Boise, Idaho spoke them in April of 2004. I worked for the Boise School District as a behavior interventionist, and had been working with a fourth grade boy who had lots of behavior problems. I was surprised that an assignment change would come with the school year coming to a close in six weeks.

"There is an emergency situation at the junior high and you are to be part of the team that is being put together." I was honored that my supervisor had selected me to help put out this fire. On the other hand, I was disappointed in having to leave my fourth grader. We had made wonderful progress in building a relationship, and were preparing a special project on the three largest snakes in the world. We had spent a lot of time researching, designing, and creating a poster for my student's presentation. "Can I say goodbye to my student and his class?" "Yes, but make it quick. They need you up there now." The principal thanked me for the work I had done at his school. I said my good byes and encouraged my student to continue practicing his presentation. I later found out that he did a good job on his report.

On my way to the junior high, I pondered what the new junior high boy would be like. I had worked with 15 to 20 boys in the previous three years. My supervisor had assigned some students, and principals had assigned others. I had also worked in self-contained portables with up to eight students. There had only been one boy where I felt that I had been unsuccessful in improving his behavior. Coincidentally, I met that "one" at the junior high two years later and he gave me a "Hi Mr. L." and a big hug. Maybe I did reach him after all!

I arrived at the junior high and ventured into the main office where I was directed to see the vice-principal. I said that I was being reassigned and was reporting there to work with a student, and he replied, "Oh good, you're here for Charlotte." Charlotte? That sounds like a girl's name. Did I hear him right? He began to fill me in a little bit about Charlotte Tate. She has autism, is non-verbal, and is very aggressive. I noticed sweat beads forming on his brow and a sense of anxiety exuding from his person. The vice-principal was a strong looking man probably in his late forties. I later found out that he had played running back for the Boise State University Broncos, the New York Jets, and the Toronto Argonauts. How could a girl's behavior affect these bodily responses from a man of his physical stature? He explained that a whole new program was being designed to facilitate the effort of working with Charlotte. A special, five-member team was being formed to work with her for the remainder of the school year. Charlotte wouldn't be returning to school until the following week. We had three days to prepare for her return. The vice-principal told me to go to room 17 where another behavior interventionist would continue the briefing.

I entered the room and recognized a colleague whom I hadn't seen in a while. Gary Washington had been permanently assigned to Charlotte and was out of the regular loop of behavior interventionists. Gary weighed about 260 pounds and was six feet tall. He was a weightlifter and enjoyed the martial arts. He had participated in professional boxing and extreme fighting. He is the kind of guy you would want on your side in the event of an altercation. He is a gentle giant, with a farm boy type of personality.

Gary explained that room 17, a full sized classroom, was being dedicated solely to Charlotte. In addition to the two of us, there would be a consulting teacher, one of Charlotte's former grade school teachers, and an occupational therapist on the team. Wow, there were five adults for one student. What was I getting myself into?

Gary continued to tell me about Charlotte. She was a seventh grader and had been in a special education classroom along with two to three other students with autism. Charlotte had behavioral problems, usually on a daily basis. Most were in the form of aggression toward staff and other students in the classroom. At other times the aggression was targeted toward herself in the form of Self-Injurious Behaviors (SIB). Charlotte was an aggressive person with a very short fuse. Her behavior would escalate in an instant and she would be inconsolable until she calmed down, which usually took between 10 and 20 minutes. Some escalations lasted as long as 45 minutes. She wouldn't hesitate to hit, grab, bite, scratch, pull hair, pinch, squeeze, head butt, or push the target of her anger. Her parents had been called numerous times throughout the year to pick up Charlotte due to her behavior at school.

The Boise School District had brought in an autism expert as a consultant in an effort to design an environment that would be conducive to helping Charlotte improve her behavior. Tom Weddle, of Spokane, Washington, recommended the changes that would be implemented by the district for the following year. A self-contained portable would be utilized for her eighth grade year, but room 17 would have to do until then.

Gary explained more about Charlotte's behavior. She had obsessive–compulsive tendencies that manifested themselves in various ways. Charlotte would repeatedly walk around the room in certain patterns.

She would take off her shoes, walk around a table, put her shoes back on, walk some more, take off the shoes, and then sit down to do work. This pattern would be replayed throughout the day. Grounding herself (getting on the ground with her knees bent and her head down) was a common occurrence. I learned not to get offended if she walked by me and didn't look at me. She would blow everyone off like that. She would also flap her arms and snap her fingers. Lots of people with autism do that as stimulation. She was very controlling of the TV and VCR. She would escalate if the video had not been rewound. No one could mess with the videos. She was the one who put them in and took them out. Also, she might take off her clothes when she was stressed out. It wasn't uncommon for her to pick her nose in front of people or put her hands down the front or back of her pants. People with autism often lack in some social graces and are carefree about attending to bodily desires.

I learned that there had been battles between Charlotte and the vice-principal, Gary, and another special education aide who was a big guy with a martial arts background. Many of the behavior escalations had to do with Charlotte wanting to control her environment. Sometimes, in order to prevent Charlotte from hurting herself or others, Gary and the other aide would place her in a therapeutic hold in order to restrain her. Training on the various therapeutic maneuvers was provided to district employees, and yearly re-certification is required. Gary said that physically restraining Charlotte was a difficult task even for two men. She was very strong and flexible, and could usually escape from the holds. After escaping, Charlotte would chase her adversary around the room until she either caught them or until she calmed down. Once again, I was asking myself what I was getting into.

Later that day, I met the consulting teacher, Sherri. She had been Charlotte's summer school teacher and had a good relationship with her. The other two members of the team came in the following morning. Jill was the occupational therapist, and Melinda had been Charlotte's special education teacher in grade school. Part of the plan was to have familiar faces around. For the next few days, we discussed how we were going to implement the program to help Charlotte with her behavior. How was her schedule going to look? What would be the room arrangement? What activities were we going to do? What would we do in the event of an escalation? For my part, I decided to get smart on autism. I got on the Internet and checked out many web sites.

Autism is a severe form of a broader group of disorders referred to as Pervasive Development Disorder (PDD). These disorders, which have their onset in childhood, include Autistic Disorder, Rett's Disorder, Childhood Disintegrative Disorder, Asperger's Syndrome, and Pervasive Developmental Disorder not otherwise specified. Sometimes teachers use the term Autism Spectrum Disorder (ASD), in referring to some or all of these five disorders. Autism, with the highest prevalence of the five disorders is the one encountered most frequently in school settings. There are seven distinct characteristics associated with autism: 1) delayed language development, 2) delayed social development, 3) repetitive behavior, 4) inappropriate behavior, 5) the need for environmental predictability, 6) sensory and movement disorders, and 7) sub-standard intellectual functioning. It appeared that Charlotte could be described as having "classic" autism.

Chapter 2

THE ROOM WAS READY AND the team was versed on what was supposed to take place. Charlotte arrived at school on Monday morning. She had a reduced hour schedule, starting at 7:25 and ending at 10:45. She entered the room and slowly evaluated her new school environment. A glaring gaze was directed at the five adults huddled on the side of the room. Charlotte was a big girl, about five foot eight, weighed 150 pounds, and was pretty athletic looking. She was also very attractive with a flawless complexion, shoulder length brown hair, and strikingly beautiful, blue eyes.

Sherri took the lead and directed Charlotte to the picture schedule. This was made up of small icon pictures velcroed to a long sheet of laminated paper. The icons indicated various activities such as "music", "relax", "movie", "story time", "art", "one on one instruction", and "deskwork". Charlotte was very familiar with this arrangement. She would start at the top and begin the first activity. After a specified amount of time, Sherri would ring a chime and Charlotte would transition to the next activity. One of the goals was to have Charlotte work with each of the five members of the team on a daily basis. This was important so that Charlotte could learn to generalize her skills between topics and instructors. While one person worked with Charlotte, the other four members talked in quiet voices and minimized their movement. There was also peaceful music playing in the background. It was a very serene environment.

When the schedule indicated that it was story time, I volunteered to read to Charlotte. I selected a book about farm animals and got some plastic farm animals to utilize while reading. Charlotte grabbed the book from me and started to flip through the pages. Some pages received a backhand slap, while others got an approving tongue licking. Then she let me share the book and read it with her. For each animal in the book, I retrieved the plastic version and made the appropriate animal sound. To my amazement, Charlotte looked me in the eye and mimicked the animal sound. We did this for each animal and it seemed like she was having fun. I had my first success with Miss Charlotte Tate.

After a few more activities, Charlotte was presented with the "movie" card. She could choose between five videos. Once a selection was made, she would put it in the VCR and turn on the TV. Gary had previously verified that all the videos had been rewound and that the TV was set to channel three. He told the team members that any variation in her "movie routine" could lead to an escalation. Charlotte would watch the movie for 10 to 15 minutes, then Sherri would ring the chimes. Charlotte would then jump up, remove the tape, and turn off the TV. Next she would check the schedule and get ready for the following subject.

On that first day, Charlotte followed the schedule and there were no escalations. However, she was very anxious at times as evidenced by her obsessive-compulsive routines. These routines centered on taking her shoes off, walking around the classroom, putting the shoes on, crawling under the table, taking the shoes off, and then sitting at her desk. It seemed that she needed to do these routines to bring order to her chaos. I got exhausted just watching her. Sometimes she would pull back the heavy couch, walk around it, push it back, then sit down to watch a movie. When the video credits rolled, she would stand on her tiptoes and do some arm flapping. When she did this, she was able to make her fingers snap together. The flapping would continue until the last credit rolled. Sometimes, during a favorite part in a video, Charlotte would flap her hand on the TV screen.

The mood had been pretty intense throughout the day. No one knew how Charlotte would react to her new surroundings and the "five adult" program. We were walking on eggshells to avoid upsetting Charlotte and the escalation that would surely follow any upset. But as a whole, that first day went pretty well.

After Charlotte left on the bus, the five of us had a meeting to discuss the day's happenings. To ease some of the built up stress, I fashioned a button that read, "I survived area 17!" We had a little chuckle and got down to business discussing the day and preparing for the next.

CHAPTER 3

I TRY TO CONNECT WITH my assigned students in a variety of ways. Many times I'll play sports with them, give out collector cards for football, basketball, baseball, and hockey, or talk about movies. How could I connect with Miss Tate? The farm animal sounds worked nicely, but I wasn't about to demean her by mooing to her on a regular basis. I decided to use SpongeBob Squarepants.

I had used SpongeBob successfully with elementary kids. I am not an artist. My drawings look very similar to what I drew 40 years ago. But for some reason, I can look at the SpongeBob characters and draw fairly good renditions. When people tell me that I am a good artist, I say, "No, artists create, I copy." There is a big difference. Anyhow, I once drew a SpongeBob for one of my elementary students, and the next thing I knew, I had orders for five more from other students who saw my "masterpiece." "Can you draw Patrick Star? Mr. Krabs?" I ended up drawing about 20 more pictures during the next few weeks.

With Charlotte, I decided to go "big time" and prior to her arrival, I drew a SpongeBob underwater scene on a white board. Part of my thought process was to see if she noticed it, and if so, if she liked it. Both questions were answered quickly. Charlotte walked to the board and picked up a yellow marker. She colored in the yellow to complete SpongeBob. She got other markers and appropriately colored in rocks, grass, and seaweed. She stayed within the lines pretty well. When she was done, she grabbed the eraser and erased the entire masterpiece. Oh well, at least she liked it. The activity put a smile on Charlotte's face and it was a nice way to start out the day. I deemed the activity a success and thought she would enjoy doing it again. However, I noticed that each day she seemed less interested, coloring fewer and fewer items. After a week, she came into the classroom, looked at the new drawing on the whiteboard, and erased it without adding her coloring. After she did the same thing the following day, I decided it was time to say adios to SpongeBob.

CHAPTER 4

CHARLOTTE PARTICULARLY LIKED DOING ARTS and crafts projects. Whether it was gluing, stapling, coloring, or cutting and pasting, she was very attentive and focused. Once a project was completed, she would exit the room, find and open her locker, put the item in her backpack, and then slam her locker shut. This would also happen when she completed her deskwork activities. The majority of the time, the hallways were empty so the locker slam echoed throughout. Those in nearby classrooms always knew when Charlotte had finished an assignment or project.

Miss Tate had a need to have closure to her activities. There must be a visible start and end to everything. And when it came to doors, they needed to be closed. If a classroom door was open, Charlotte couldn't walk by without swinging it shut. This slamming became an annoyance to some teachers due to the jolting effect it provided on the students in the classroom. Gary and I would attempt to grab the door to avoid the slam but were not always successful. The teachers would come out with a scowl on their faces, and we would just smile and say, "Sorry." Charlotte also liked to close the big hallway doors. They would slowly make their way to the closure point and all the while, Charlotte would be watching intently, flapping her arm and hand in the air until the door had shut completely.

The days went pretty smoothly, with Charlotte following the picture schedule fairly well. However, there were a few escalations and many aggressions toward teachers in the form of hitting or slugging. Charlotte would walk by a seated or standing adult and whack them on the shoulder or arm. When Charlotte whacked, pinched, or grabbed someone, a contusion was sure to appear the following day. We kept a log of every aggression or escalation. It was called the ABC log (Antecedent, Behavior, and Consequence). A detailed account was required for each incident. After three weeks, there had been a total of 4 major escalations, 88 incidences of hitting teachers, and 10 Self-Injurious Behaviors (SIB) observed.

On one of those occasions of aggression, Charlotte demonstrated full awareness of a higher thinking process. Charlotte was upset with something and was walking behind Jill. She suddenly whacked Jill in the shoulder and continued walking. Jill remarked, "Thanks Charlotte." Charlotte immediately turned around, returned to Jill, and whacked her again on the shoulder. I suppressed a giggle because of the implication that Charlotte was aware of Jill's sarcasm and hadn't appreciated the comment. I started to view Miss Tate a little differently after that episode. She had great receptive language, and possibly a higher intellect than educators had observed in the past.

Later that day I asked Charlotte to get some scissors, glue, and a pencil for an art project. She immediately retrieved those items from her desk. This further confirmed in my mind that she easily understood spoken language. I walked up to her and whispered in her ear, "I know you can understand me." She looked at me directly, eye to eye. Her intelligence, comprehension, and awareness were irrefutable. While Charlotte might have challenging behaviors, I was now keenly aware that she was also a human being, not a wild animal.

I had reviewed her previous incident reports, all of which backed up the "wild animal" description. There was page after page of escalations and incidents. There had been hitting, scratching, pulling hair, pinching, biting, grabbing, pulling fingers backwards, head butting, and kicking. From the get go in the public school system, Charlotte had demonstrated aggressive behaviors toward principals, vice principals, teachers, special education aides, youth companions, behavior interventionists, and other students. Many reports indicated that Charlotte also would turn her aggression toward herself. She would hit herself violently in the head or thighs with her fists. She might bang her head against a wall or a window, and occasionally, this behavior would result in a broken window. Many of these SIB would come after an aggression toward another person. I hypothesized that she was punishing herself for her actions. Maybe she knew that it was wrong to hit other people, but she just couldn't stop herself from doing it.

My first experience of a major escalation occurred after Charlotte completed an art project. She didn't want to let the glue dry prior to putting the project in her backpack. It totally fell apart. Charlotte became quite upset. She got loud vocally in the hallway and slammed her locker. She got a drink and calmly returned to the room. But upon her return, she promptly hit Gary three times in the chest. Then she picked up a sparkly glue tube, made me her chosen target, and I got whacked with the glue tube on my shoulder. The glue squirted all over her hand and shirt. Now she was really upset and marched off to the bathroom to wash off that negative tactile stimulation. The hallways echoed with her loud vocal noises. Jill ventured into the bathroom while Gary and I remained outside. Charlotte was unable to turn off the water and Jill asked if she needed some help. Charlotte replied physically by hitting Jill on the shoulder and then pulling her hair. She head butted Jill two times and then held Jill's head with both hands and pressed her forehead against Jill's. This lasted almost twenty seconds, during which time Charlotte was gritting her teeth and straining her facial muscles. Charlotte's attention returned to the running water. Closure of this activity had yet to be accomplished. She tried to turn the water off, but without success. Again Jill asked if she needed help. Charlotte was annoyed at the repetition of this question and placed Jill in a headlock. She head butted her two more times. Satisfied that her response was now getting through to Jill, Charlotte returned to the sink and managed to turn off the faucet. She then returned to the room with Gary and I following. The other classroom adults were in front of the door along with Walter, the in-house detention supervisor, who had heard the commotion and had come to help. Charlotte smacked Walter and then pounded on the lockers very loudly. Upon entering the room, Sherri gave her a movie card and it was accepted. While watching the movie, *Anastasia*, Charlotte finally calmed down.

Sherri decided to call Phil Tate, Charlotte's father, to pick her up. He owned a manufacturing business about five minutes away. There was little hope of Charlotte having a productive day after that escalation and there was a concern that there might be a problem if she took the bus home. I had not met dad and was looking forward to doing so. When Phil Tate came in, Charlotte's mood changed immediately. He greeted her with a loud, "Hey Chuck, what's up?" I thought we were supposed to speak in soft voices around Charlotte. She looked at dad and tilted her head slightly, quizzing him with her eyes as to what was going to happen. He continued to talk in a regular voice level and said that they were going to go home. Introductions were made and an explanation was given as to what had transpired. After observing Phil for a few minutes, I realized that he would be my perfect roll model. Talk and act like a regular person when interfacing with Charlotte. Treat her age appropriately, just like any other 14-year-old teenager. These two behaviors on my part would help allow for a marvelous relationship to develop.

In an effort to avoid provoking an escalation, part of the plan would be to allow Charlotte the freedom to leave the room to get a drink of water or go to the bathroom whenever she wanted. Previously, Charlotte was not allowed to leave the room unless Gary or I escorted her. That frequently led to behavior escalations. Lots of times Charlotte would want to venture out as the other students were transitioning between classes. This could potentially pose problems for Gary and me. He would walk on the side or in front of Charlotte and I would follow from a short distance behind. Most of the kids knew about Charlotte's unusual behaviors such as locker slamming, loud guttural noises, or possibly escalations outside of the classroom. Kids moved out of her way as they looked at the "autistic" girl coming toward them. That helped us a lot by clearing a pathway. Many times, however, Charlotte would drop down in a busy hallway and assume her grounding "praying to Mecca" position. We then had to protect her from getting trampled by the mass of students. Needless to say, the grounding activity drew lots of puzzled looks from her peers and faculty members alike. We'd breathe a sigh of relief whenever those adventures turned out to be uneventful.

We began to anticipate potential problems whenever Charlotte wanted to leave the classroom while other students were in the hallways. Most of the time, she just wanted to get a drink of water. Once she had pushed another student out of the way while he was drinking from the fountain. After that, Gary and I would take turns standing by the fountain prior to the class-ending bell. We'd strongly encourage kids to drink up and move away when Charlotte appeared in the hallway. This was a successful intervention and no other problems occurred as a result of a congested drinking fountain.

I decided to see how far our relationship had grown by testing Charlotte's proximity comfort level. When she was watching a movie, she was queen of the couch. It was inadvisable to sit next to her unless you wanted to risk getting booted off, or worse, experiencing a video time escalation. At first I just stood by one of the armrests, and watched the movie. She tolerated my presence. I did this a few more times and there were no problems. Next I sat down on the side of the couch, laying my arm on the armrest. Charlotte looked at me and made one of her noises. I didn't budge and continued to act like I belonged there. Charlotte continued to make her negative noises in conjunction with moving her foot toward the armrest. Next, she "toed" me, pushing my arm off the couch with her toes. I left my arm off, but remained seated. She began watching the movie again. Progress had been made. In the next few days, I felt brave enough to actually sit on the armrest. The first few times she vocalized disapproval and "toed" me off quickly. There was no aggression, so I continued to try until she finally accepted my keister on the armrest of her couch. After a few minutes of this toleration, she realized what I had accomplished, and I got the toe treatment. I was satisfied with my success and didn't push it any farther.

CHAPTER 5

WHAT TURNED OUT TO BE Charlotte's final day of school started out like all the rest.... following the schedule. Charlotte would usually begin the day with proper behaviors. As the day wore on, she would scrutinize her schedule and at times, remove the icons that she did not want in her plans for that day. We would sneak them back in when we could. This didn't faze Miss Tate, as she would just remove them again and file them behind a bookshelf.

Hours before the end of the school day, Charlotte decided it was time to go home on the bus. She walked out of the room and got her backpack. Gary and I followed her down the hallway and out of the building. We tried to reason with her to return to class, but to no avail. She started to get verbally loud, making her guttural noises that would reverberate through our bodies and prepare us mentally for a possible escalation. She finally accepted redirection and returned to the classroom, but she was making her noises continually as she went down the hallway. Teachers were preemptively closing their doors. Charlotte and the five adults were now outside of room 17 and Charlotte would not enter. I said to her in a calm voice, "Let's sit down," and I sat down on the floor. She did the same and seemed to calm down a little bit. She quickly stood up and I arose too. Then the calmness left her and she got loud again. She was standing about five feet from me. She stared directly at me and raised her right arm high in the air. She was on her tiptoes, and it seemed to me that her fist was near the ceiling. Since that moment, I believe that I know what a nail feels like just before the hammer comes down. Something deep inside me remembered some training that I had been given years before. Stay calm, don't escalate yourself, put your hands out with the palms down, and say "No hit, no hit." I did all of those things as Charlotte prepared to pound me. She hesitated for a couple of seconds and evidently processed some thoughts. She returned to standing flat-footed and brought her arm down from the ceiling. She continued to look at my eyes. At that point, she slapped me softly with her open hand three times on the shoulder. But I knew I had been spared her wrath when she quickly turned toward Gary. He would not be so fortunate. She went after him with multiple blows from both the left and the right. After hitting Gary, she again got her backpack and headed down the hallway. Gary and I tried to explain that the bus wouldn't be coming for some time. She ignored our logic and continued to head for the bus stop. After staying with her for a few minutes, Gary said it was time to escort her back to the classroom. He said he would take the lead and for me to follow. He placed her in a one-arm escort hold and began to make the trek down the hallway. Charlotte was able to bring her head around over his shoulder. Her long brown hair concealed her face and head from my vantagepoint. Her head remained there for most of the escort. Gary's face was kind of red and he was grimacing, but he asked for no assistance. He got her into the room and released the hold. Charlotte bolted away toward her couch. Gary examined his back and found four sets of teeth marks. He went to the nurse for first aid. Charlotte's behavior that day was unacceptable and earned her an early summer vacation from school.

CHAPTER 6

CHARLOTTE'S PREVIOUS TEACHER HAD RAISED the question of labeling her disability. Did she have autism, another disability, or a combination? The district asked for and received permission from the Tates to have Charlotte evaluated. This took place in the middle of June 2004.

Charlotte and Phil flew to Denver, Colorado and checked into the Psychiatric Special Care Unit of The Children's Hospital on the campus of The University of Colorado. She would be assessed for her aggression in order to stabilize her escalating aggressive behaviors, which would allow for a safe return to a school setting. Another part of the evaluation would include a mental status examination. In order to rule out the existence of certain disabilities, there would also be analysis of DNA, organic and amino acids, creatine levels, and phenylalanine/tyrosine levels. Finally, an MRI of Charlotte's brain, and an electroencephalogram would be administered.

The Mental Status Examination provided little new information. She was essentially non-verbal and slapped her fingers when working on a computer. She used a picture schedule and enjoyed children's books. There was an absence of eye contact and any appropriate interpersonal reciprocal communication skills. She had a very strict demand for routines and most, if not all of her aggressive outbursts were associated with interference of those routines. Judgement and insight were deemed completely absent.

The results of the High-Resolution Chromosome study and DNA for Fragile X syndrome were negative. Organic and amino acids, creatine, and the phenylalanine/tyrosine levels were all reported as normal. The MRI of her brain and the electroencephalogram were both reported as normal.

Charlotte tolerated the psychopharmacologic interventions very well. She would begin taking the anti-obsessive antidepressant medication, Fluoxetine, which would target her significant obsessive-compulsive disorder features. She would also receive Trazadone to help her sleep or to calm her down when she was agitated.

Charlotte's discharge diagnosis included Obsessive-Compulsive Disorder (severe), Major Depressive Disorder, Autistic Disorders, and moderate cognitive impairment.

There would be no summer school for her that year. Her parents had decided that a break from school would probably be a good thing. I was asked if I would work with Miss Tate for her eighth grade year in the new environment that was currently being created on the junior high campus. The new classroom consisted of two doublewide portables that had two bathrooms, a kitchen, a classroom area, and a TV/relaxation area. There would also be a time out room. This self-contained classroom would be used for junior high students who fall under the umbrella of the autism spectrum.

As I pondered my decision to work with Charlotte, I reflected on how I had been spared the hammer/nail pounding in the hallway. She was very escalated at the time, but still managed to have cognitive thought processes. She didn't want to hurt me but she still needed to whack me a little. I knew that somewhere inside her, she choose to show me mercy. Did she see something in me that had been absent from aides, teachers, and others that had worked with her during her lifetime? I felt that this unreachable, unteachable kid could indeed be reachable and teachable. I would step up to the plate.

I had lots of time to think about working with Charlotte over my summer vacation. My primary responsibility would be to help her with her behaviors, although I found the challenge of being her one on one aide/helper/teacher to be fascinating. I was not a certified teacher and had no experience working with people with autism except for my work with Charlotte. At that point, I only had moderate success, but there was success, and I deeply believed there could be more.

Over the summer, I read a couple of books on autism. I read The Curious Incident of the Dog in the Night-Time and The Mind Tree: A Miraculous Child Breaks the Silence of Autism. Both books gave me some valuable insight into the mind of an autistic person.

As the summer vacation was drawing to a close, I began to get anxious about the upcoming year. Sure, I had some success working with Charlotte. I also had confidence in my abilities to deescalate a situation without utilizing physical intervention. I was somewhat apprehensive about going into battle day after day. I had received bruises and scratches from Charlotte that had lasted days. How could I look forward to working with one of the toughest students in the district? I actually had a few nightmares about it. There were a few nights when my brain wouldn't shut down and I tossed and turned for seemingly unending hours. I did have one positive dream, which helped calm my concerns and give me some direction and possible goals. In my dream, Charlotte was talking like everyone else. We were having a conversation and I was telling her that her words and sentences sounded great. This dream would help inspire me during the next two years.

CHAPTER 7

PRIOR TO THE FIRST DAY of eighth grade, I met with the special education teacher who would be in charge of the new classroom. Mr. D. Thomas had transferred from another school district to start the new program. He had lots of previous experience working with kids who had disabilities. He said that we would be starting out with four students and that number could change during the year. Two of the students had been with Charlotte prior to her reassignment to room 17. Another girl had been with Charlotte at an elementary school program. We would be starting the year with the new teacher, two special education aides, and myself. I would be Charlotte's one on one aide. My focus would be on helping Charlotte's behavior. There was no set curriculum for me to use. I would have to find out her interests and strengths and then incorporate them into teaching moments.

I again reviewed some of the vast files that had been garnered about Miss Tate. I tried to see if there were certain triggers that preceded escalations. I had no luck. Time of day, time between eating, requests to do work, and other variables were analyzed. There were no patterns of consistency. In fact, the only consistent thing about Charlotte's escalations and incidents was the inconsistency. Randomness ruled.

Some of the notes indicated that she liked Disney movies and coloring pages. We had some resource materials with Disney themes. Some were coloring pages and others were more functional matching activities. These had pictures of the Disney characters and matching names of the characters. There were other materials that I thought I could use if Charlotte was interested.

Charlotte was scheduled to begin school about 9:00 and leave at 2:00. This schedule allowed the bus company to dedicate a bus for Charlotte, as she had had some incidents on the bus in the past. There would also be a familiar bus driver and an adult aide on the bus in an effort to minimize potential problems.

The first few weeks of eighth grade went very smoothly as Charlotte adjusted to her new school environment. We utilized a new picture icon schedule for the various activities of the day. Initially she followed the schedule nicely. In time, however, she returned to her old trick of removing her least favorite icons and filing them behind a bookshelf. I was fine with this because it empowered her to have some control over her day and to make choices. Charlotte was typing on her portable dictionary device quite a bit. I would give her 20 flashcards and she would follow the same routine with each word…1) Open the cover, 2) turn on the device, 3) type the word, 4) hit the enter button, 5) look at the word's on-screen meaning, 6) turn off the device, 7) shut the cover. This routine would be repeated time and time again for each flashcard. I tried to model some shortcuts like not opening and shutting the cover and hitting the "clear" button prior to entering a new word. Charlotte would vocalize her opposition to my suggestions, so I desisted. I was trained to evaluate situations by using the "so what" principle. If behaviors were minor and didn't really matter that much, it could be classified as a "so what." I would use this qualifier almost every day.

Charlotte was still demonstrating some old behaviors. She would push out her chair and walk around her desk after completing an assignment. After that, she would leave the room and go outside to a nearby grid, tear up the assignment and shove the paper down through the bars. This was her filing system and none of my logical redirections would get through to her. This behavior would happen after each completed assignment whether it was a cut and paste matching worksheet, coloring page, or another activity. This could happen up to 20 times a day. At first I would stand outside and verify that the grid was her destination and that she would return to the classroom. After a few days of this unchanging routine, I would stand at the window and watch from inside. After a few more days, I would stay seated and await her return. After a few weeks, I removed the grid and climbed down to gather up the mountain of work.

Mr. Thomas decided that we should try to reshape this behavior and he acquired an extra garbage can to be placed on our landing area. He cut some rectangular openings in the lid to simulate a grid. The hope was to get Charlotte to discard her assignments in this container rather than the original grid. Charlotte would walk right by this crude simulation of her "filing system" on the way to the original grid. Next we tried wedging paper into the lid's openings and I demonstrated the proper procedure for discarding papers. Eventually, Charlotte would push my papers down, but would still dispose of her papers in the original grid. Finally one day she used the garbage can to "file" her assignment. She repeated this procedure more and more. She finally stopped going to the grid altogether. Another success!

Another one of her old behaviors had to do with glue sticks. After using a new glue stick, she would twist the dial until the column of glue would arise from the tube. Charlotte would then grab the exposed tower of glue and toss it in the garbage can. I treated this as a "so what" until we burned through three boxes of glue sticks in one week. From then on, I held the glue stick and doled out little chunks as needed. This was a great opportunity to have her vocalize her needs. Previously, Charlotte had only initiated the word "sharpen" when she was using colored pencils.

While holding the glue stick, I waited until she said "glue please" prior to giving it to her. I only had to model the phrase a few times before she understood and mimicked me. It was exciting to hear her use appropriate language and it gave me great pleasure to know that I was helping her to communicate.

Whenever she was doing independent activities, I tried to incorporate some one on one interaction. When we did cut and paste activities, I would have her do the first rough-cut with scissors. I would then wait for her to hand it to me to do the fine cutting. She was making lots of eye contact during these activities.

I was feeling pretty darn good about our positive working relationship. There had been only three minor escalations during those first two weeks of eighth grade. Previously, she could have had as many as three or more escalations daily. We continued to implement our semi-structured days for the remainder of August. I would set up the icons for the day and Charlotte would tweak the arrangement to her liking. I told her that was OK. She enjoyed popping in a video after putting her lunch and backpack away. This was how she liked to start her day. No problem Charlotte. Sometimes she would check out the work I had for her in a folder. She'd thumb through the papers, remove a few, and file them behind the bookshelf. Later, unnoticed, I would retrieve them and place them back in the folder. She'd eventually find them and would again deposit them behind the bookshelf. When she had removed them twice, I pretty much got the message. She was obviously communicating her desire not to do these activities.

After watching a video for a few minutes, Charlotte would come to the other room and do some coloring. She would position herself so she could crane her neck to see the TV through the hallway between the two portables. This would assure her that no one had messed with the TV or VCR. She would continue to do her work just fine as long as she knew the TV was on. When I told her mom, Angie Tate, that we were allowing her to leave the TV on while she worked, she was so happy that we weren't using the TV time as a reward or taking it away as punishment. TV was a major leisure activity for Charlotte and was often an antecedent for an escalation when Charlotte lost control of her viewing. We chose to eliminate that anxiety by letting Charlotte run the TV and VCR throughout the day. When the other students objected or tried to change programs, Charlotte would begin to audibly escalate until I intervened. I explained to the students that we didn't want Charlotte to get mad and they seemed to accept the necessity for the "Charlotte rule."

Charlotte's head banging and pounding her fists against objects continued to be a concern. It was hard to watch when she would hit her head against doors, walls, windows, computers, or bookshelves. There were times when I thought she might knock herself out. We were also deeply concerned when she would pound on the top of the computer monitor or on the glass screen. We felt there might have been an explosion if she had managed to break through the glass. As an intervention, Mr. Thomas ordered special computer containment furniture to be built by a special education work program. This furniture would fit snuggly around the hard drive and monitor so they couldn't be hit directly. In addition, I kept Charlotte away from the computer by not allowing it during her school day for a period of time. For the most part, she left it alone. She did enjoy watching the other students operate it, however, and that seemed to pacify her.

Charlotte was allowed to venture into the main building if she so desired. I would grab a two-way radio whenever we left our classroom. Her favorite destination was the library. She would go to the video shelf and select a movie. At first the librarians were somewhat apprehensive about having her in "their" space. Charlotte's reputation was known to all, and they didn't want any disruptions. Everyone knows that you need to be quiet in a library and that could sometimes be hard for Charlotte. I felt it was important for Charlotte to feel comfortable when she left the portable, and the library was a happy destination for her. It was also important for her to be with and see other kids. I encouraged her to go often and she did. She would get a movie and watch it for 15 minutes. She'd loose interest and we'd return the video to the library only to get another one. After a short period of time, she would loose interest in the new video and the routine would be repeated. This happened four or five times daily for a week. Like many things with Charlotte, this behavior would self-extinguish after a time. During the library phase, Charlotte behaved appropriately and had no flare-ups. The librarians were impressed with her behavior and invited her back graciously.

There was one scary moment toward the end of September. Charlotte had been relaxing on the floor when she suddenly popped up. She obtained a pair of scissors and began to cut a lock of her hair from the back of her head. After doing that, she threw the hair away, put the scissors on the counter, and sat down near the door. For no apparent reason, she began to get upset. She got up and retrieved the scissors. She now was beginning to escalate and looked almost tormented. She had the scissors in her hand and was making loud noises. She turned to the wall and quickly stabbed it five times below the clock. She then turned toward me. As she approached me, I was unsure of her intentions. She was still pretty agitated, but I sensed no animosity toward me. In a calm and steady voice, I directed her to "Put the scissors down." She hesitated, then held out her arm to me. I took the scissors and tossed them toward Mr. Thomas who was behind me. Charlotte grabbed my arm and was opening her mouth. She had never tried to bite me before, and I certainly didn't want her to develop a new behavior like that. I got my arm out of her grasp and said, "No biting!" a few times. She then returned to the area where she had been relaxing, but not before she hit the bookshelves three times really hard. We decided that all scissors should go into a faculty storage closet from then on. Charlotte calmed quickly and was fine the rest of the day. Mr. Thomas and I discussed the incident after school. He said he was under the impression that her intent was to stab me and maybe it had something to do with her medication. I disagreed. If she had wanted to aerate me, she would have come at me with a raised arm like when she stabbed the wall. I knew from past experiences that Charlotte was predictable when it came to hitting. It was always a big overhand right blow. She had approached me with the right arm bent at the elbow, scissors in her hand. I never felt threatened during that incident. Before leaving that day, I examined the five stab marks in the wall......Nice grouping!

We only had to call Phil or Angie once to pick Charlotte up early during that first month. Luckily it was not for an aggressive episode. Charlotte was watching TV when the bus arrived and refused to leave the room. She wanted to finish the program she was watching. We decided not to force her onto the bus for fear of provoking an escalation and endangering the bus personnel. Charlotte was allowed to finish her show and Angie picked her up 45 minutes after the bus had departed.

Chapter 8

Charlotte had continued her good work ethic, completing at least eight out of ten activities or worksheets during the day. She could easily match the correct color that was prompted for use on a coloring activity. Some days she would do the coloring activity, then go to my work folder and grab five more of the same activity. She'd complete them all. Of course, these completed sheets of paper would be torn up and deposited in the grated garbage can outside the room. Every now and then, she'd venture to the original grid and push the worksheets through. One day, to my complete surprise, Charlotte handed me a completed assignment. I looked it over, then promptly walked to our work display corkboard and tacked it up for all to see. I was proud of her and she also seemed proud to have her work up with the other students' work.

In October, Charlotte developed a fixation with the heating vent grill on the side of a wall near the TV. For some unexplained reason, the previous allure of the grid and garbage can grate had diminished. Now, all her completed work had to be stuffed through this much smaller heating vent grill. This might have been a "so what" except that an accumulation of paper there might have posed a fire hazard. There was a ledge behind the grill that held the stuffed-in papers and Charlotte didn't like to see anything remaining. She would blow the papers until they disappeared behind the wall. After school I would unscrew the grill and remove the papers.

One day Charlotte was having a hard time with a piece of paper that was refusing to skinny up and go through the grill. She was starting to get upset, then stopped and grabbed my hand. She put my hand on the stubborn paper. I got the message and pushed it through. She got some more papers and gave them to me. I decided to play dumb and gestured, "What?" with my palms up. I didn't really want to foster this new obsession, but I didn't want her to escalate either. She pushed my hand near the vent and I complied by pushing the papers through. Charlotte needed to see these papers disappear in order to fulfill her closure requirement. She blew air through the grill, but the papers only moved slightly. She then pounded the grill with her fist and it responded by bending in and reshaping itself. I quickly intervened by saying, "Mr. Dean help." Charlotte stopped. I decided to use this as a teaching moment and told her we were going to count to three, then blow the papers away. She pronounced "one, two, three" with me. Then we both took a breath and blew into the vent. I was thrilled that some of the papers responded to our blast and moved away from our view. We repeated this a few more times until most of the papers were out of view. There was still one piece that was positioned beneath a lip in the vent and refused to budge. Charlotte wanted this one out of sight too. I tried blowing again but was unsuccessful. This did not sit well with Charlotte and she started grabbing and slapping at my arms. I blocked a slap to my face and held my ground saying, "No hitting." She stopped, then put my hand on the vent again. I tried once more to blow it away to no avail. She immediately returned to the slapping and grabbing behavior. One of the other students came over to help out. Unfortunately, Sam, who weighed about 250 pounds, stepped on one of Charlotte's fingers.

This did not contribute to de-escalating the situation at all. Charlotte again took out her anger on my arms. I loudly said, "No hitting!" She complied immediately. I left the vent area and she calmed quickly. But that afternoon, when Charlotte got on the bus, she started banging her head against the window. The bus driver didn't want to leave due to safety concerns. We decided to call her parents to take her home.

The next day, Charlotte deposited some papers into the heating vent. She tried to blow them by herself, but was unsuccessful and began to get upset. She came, got my hand, and escorted me to the vent. Before I attempted anything, I reminded her, "No hitting Mr. Dean." She repeated my words. I proceeded to blow the paper out of view, and Charlotte was a happy camper again.

The vent routine continued to avail itself to teaching moments. We were now counting to five together prior to blowing. I would hold up one finger, then two, etc… until we got to five. Each time I would say the number and then tap my fingers on her arm as a tactile reinforcer. This was always fun for Charlotte. We progressed to having Charlotte say the last number, five, when I hesitated after saying four. This demonstrated to me that she knew the sequences of numbers.

I began introducing questions requiring a yes/no answer. We did this on the computer with some success. I was hoping to accomplish three things: 1) appropriate use of the computer, 2) communicating appropriately, and 3) getting her used to typing answers on the computer. This could enable me to introduce more sophisticated computer communication software programs in the future. I would type out a question, then put her index finger on the "y" key for yes or the "n" key for no. She was excited and tolerated my controlling her hand movements. According to her mom, Angie, she used to type out locations that she wanted to visit on her portable typer. This ability had evidently regressed and would not be generalized with other typing devices. I was hoping to introduce the computer keyboard to help facilitate her communication, but her regression in typing skills made this difficult.

During October, Charlotte's use of spoken language was being observed more frequently than in the past. She would repeat the names of various colors after I said the name. She continued to initiate the phrase, "Glue please" appropriately and also, "Good bye" on occasion. Some people with autism have delayed speech and I was hoping that Charlotte would progress enough to avoid living in her non-verbal world.

A funny thing happened one day. Charlotte was on "her" couch watching TV when Andy, another student, came in and sat down one seat cushion away from her. She gave him a quizzical look and brought her leg up on the couch. She slowly inched her toes under Andy's bottom and he responded by moving over just a little. Charlotte continued with a grin on her face. She toed Andy until he got off the couch. By that time, Charlotte was thoroughly enjoying this game and had a huge smile on her mug. I was laughing out loud and Andy was also smiling. The whole episode lasted about 30 seconds. It was very cool to see the humor and playfulness displayed by these two kids. Charlotte would eventually let Andy on her couch without hesitation or confrontation.

Up to this point, Charlotte had escalated only a few times. There were some tense moments, but she self regulated and calmed quickly. She was having great success controlling her anger and frustration. That semi-honeymoon period would come to a standstill on October 15, 2004.

Because Charlotte was so dominating over the leisure room TV, a second TV on rollers was brought into the classroom. This was to be used for kids other than Charlotte, which gave the other students a chance to choose their movies. When Charlotte walked in from the bus, she immediately noticed the new TV in the corner. This was a change to her environment and she had not authorized anything. Although her irritation was clearly visible, she made no effort to do anything. Her plan to restore the status quo of the room would have to wait for a more appropriate time. That time would come in the late morning when only Charlotte, another aide, and I were in the classroom.

Charlotte was sitting near the TV enjoying a book. She finished the book and placed it back on the bookshelf. She then turned and walked to the new TV on rollers. She unplugged it and began rolling it toward the door. My senses were screaming, "Danger, danger!" My brain quickly envisioned a potential outcome video. I saw Charlotte trying to push the TV and stand out the door and off the landing. I saw the TV stand leaving deck and balancing on the handrail. Next, the top-heavy weight of the TV succumbed to the force of gravity and turned the stand into a catapult. I could visualize my student getting caught by the stand and turning into a human projectile, flying through the air and landing near the main building 10 yards away. This did not pass the "so what" test.

I intervened and grabbed the back of the cart. Charlotte wasn't happy with the "help" I was giving her. She got loud vocally and pulled even harder. The TV began rocking back and forth. I tried to redirect her by telling her to roll it into the kitchen area. She would have none of that and continued struggling to pull it toward the door. When I continued to pull in the opposite direction, Charlotte realized that the "Mr. Dean anchor" had to be eliminated in order for her to accomplish her goal. She stopped pulling and came after me in full fury. I let go of the TV and got ready for a donnybrook. Charlotte came toward me with arms preparing for overhead blows. She had a tendency to use her right arm first and this time would be no different. I raised my left arm over my head in a defensive position and awaited the blow. It came, but was thwarted by my left. She then let loose an arsenal of both lefts and rights. My right arm was now parroting the efforts of my left. I lost count of how many punches she had launched. I was blocking everything coming my way. Charlotte paused and round one was in the books.

The break between rounds lasted only a few seconds, hardly enough time for me to towel off and catch my breath. Then she was back to the TV stand and heading toward the door. I again began the opposing pull while verbally directing her to stop her behavior. She realized the futility of pulling the TV and once again went after the "anchor." In the meantime, the other aide was able to confiscate the TV, roll it into the kitchen area, lock both doors, and then call for backup.

Round two was essentially a replay of round one. Blow after blow from Charlotte, block after block by me, and the adrenaline was definitely flowing. I had lots of competition in high school sports 30 years before that, but nothing compared to this battle. I decided to do a one-arm hold from behind her back. I got into position and executed the maneuver. I now thought I had some physical control and continued trying to reason with Charlotte. Because she was highly escalated, Charlotte probably couldn't hear or understand me. My head was tucked down low on her back and I had control of her left arm by wrapping both my arms around her waist and holding her forearm. Charlotte began to headbutt with the back of her head, but I was too low on her back for our skulls to meet.

Time to go to the floor. From the one-armed hold, I put some pressure on her hipbone and pulled back a little. Charlotte came back with me and sat nicely on the floor. I still had the arm hold and my head was still low on her back. I continued to hold Charlotte in an effort to give her time to calm down, but she was not ready yet. I felt that I could maintain this position for a while, at least until the Calvary arrived. I was wrong to make that assumption. Charlotte is very flexible and was able to reach back with her free arm and clutch a clump of my hair. Ouch!! I released my hold, got up, and moved away. I was hoping that this momentary break and separation would allow Charlotte a chance to chill. Wrong again. She was eager to begin round three.

Again, Charlotte began throwing a barrage of rights and lefts. I continued to meet each one with my blocking forearms. Charlotte was losing steam, as her blows were less rapid. Suddenly, she broke off the combative engagement and went through the hallway to the other half of our portable. She went to the kitchen door and began pulling on the doorknob. She hadn't forgotten that the TV had been rolled in there before. At this point, I was just monitoring her behavior and following her around. The Calvary arrived in the form of Mr. Thomas, the school principal, and the vice-principal. Their presence didn't impress Charlotte very much. She turned away from the kitchen door and again began throwing punches at me. After some blocks and deflects, I directed her to her couch and she finally consented. The principals were looking at me with wide eyes. They inquired as to my health. I told them I was okay, just tired. The whole episode had lasted about 10 minutes. I excused myself to wash up. When I looked in the mirror, I realized what the principals had been looking at. My face and eyes were beet red, and I was sweating like a pig. My stomach began to react to the adrenaline and stress of the previous confrontation. I felt nauseous. I began to clean some scratches I had received during the ordeal.

Charlotte seemed equally tired as she just sat on the couch with her arms resting at her sides. The aide and I began the write-up on the events that had transpired. My hands were still shaking and it was hard to write. I sat down and rested for ten minutes. I felt a lot better after that and was able to complete the report.

It was important for me to find out where Charlotte's head was. I went to her and held out my hand. "Are we still friends?" She gave me a "five" slap on the hand and I felt good. I talked to her about the incident and explained why I couldn't let the TV leave the room. I was taking a chance that she might re-escalate. She was receptive to my conversation and remained calm. I talked a little longer, then left her alone to think about things. When she left that day, she was a calm tired kid.

CHAPTER 9

THE REMAINDER OF OCTOBER SAW Charlotte exhibiting a strong work ethic. She was completing the majority of her deskwork and activities that were planned each day. The output she produced was still getting torn up and tossed into the garbage can or the vent. That vent cover would need replacement due to an altercation with Charlotte. I had begun refusing to blow the papers away because it was enabling the "paper disposal" behavior. My non-participation resulted in Charlotte getting upset and smashing in the vent cover.

A field trip was planned just before Halloween. I had volunteered my ranch for the outing and all the kids were excited. The kids' parents were all invited too. There were horses, chickens, a turkey, a snake, and dogs to play with. We also had a pumpkin patch where the kids picked their own Halloween pumpkins. There was a nearby pond that we visited.

I had set up a calf roping event and a horseshoe hunting game. The boys enjoyed throwing a lariat and the girls found most of the horseshoes. Pizza and drinks were enjoyed by all. After everyone had left, I was thinking about how there had been no behavior incidents from any of the students. It was as if being in the country atmosphere had a soothing effect on the kids. Later, photos of the outing were mounted in our classroom, and were enjoyed by students and visitors alike.

I had a brainstorm for a new activity that I thought would be fun for Charlotte. It was making collages. I cut out various figures from coloring pages that were ocean related. On poster paper, I drew a wavy line a little above the center. Charlotte was to glue all the underwater figures such as whales, starfish, and fish under the line. Pictures of boats, the sun, and clouds were to go above the wavy line. After she glued all of the pictures in their appropriate places, she got her crayons and colored them all. She had demonstrated great awareness of knowing the proper environment for each item. This was pretty cool. I would use collages for a variety of activities in the future.

I introduced a new communication board that I called the Velcro Request Board or VRB. It was a basic design. One line of Velcro tape was near the top. This was the communication line. Velcro tape below held various icons to be used by both Charlotte and me. There were icons for pizza, popcorn, peanuts, TV, VCR, video, library, bathroom, yes, no, and lots of other things. The idea was to have Charlotte request things by placing the icon or a series of icons on the top line. I showed her how I wanted her to use the icons, but I was preaching to the choir. She was familiar with icon usage and had immediate success using the VRB. She got the video icon and placed it on the top line. I let her chose a movie and away she went.

She continued to use the VRB mainly to request food items, and I used it to prepare her for what was coming next academically. Whenever she placed an icon on the top line, I would leave it there, and add an icon for the activity that would follow. Knowing what was coming up next usually helped Charlotte transition smoothly.

CHAPTER 10

THROUGHOUT THE MONTH OF NOVEMBER, Charlotte displayed appropriate behavior while using the computer. I would pre-teach "No hitting computer!" prior to each time she used it. I could anticipate compliance when she made eye contact with me. She liked playing a concentration type game involving matching two unseen pictures. The pictures would remain face up if they were correctly matched. Otherwise they would be turned back to the face down position. Charlotte was pretty good at doing this activity. She also had the option of playing this game by matching words with the corresponding pictures. Charlotte nailed this one too, and further demonstrated her penchant for reading.

I bought Charlotte a Minnie Mouse beanie baby at a flea market and looked forward to seeing her reaction when I gave it to her. She studied it for a while and then started to dissect it. First she pulled off the legs, then the arms. She peeled back the red and white polka dot skirt to reveal Minnie's torso. Soon all the stuffing was removed and Minnie became more two-dimensional than three. Charlotte collected the assortment of body parts and materials and gave them a proper burial in the outside grid.

Later that same day, Andy was standing and rocking back and forth in front of the TV. Charlotte was beginning to get annoyed so I prompted her to say, "Move please." She said it very clearly, and Andy backed away. Way to communicate Charlotte!

Just before our Thanksgiving break, we got a visit from Tom Weddle, the district's autism consultant from Spokane, Washington. He was very pleased with our new portables and the environment that had been created. He was pleasantly surprised at how much Charlotte had progressed since his initial visit earlier in the year. She was interacting socially with people and communicating with the VRB appropriately. These were wonderful progressions for her. He was impressed with how easily I interacted with Charlotte and the way she responded to my requests to do things. When I told him that Charlotte had given me a few pieces of popcorn, Tom said, "Great, now the next thing to do is to sit on the couch with her, watch a movie, and share a whole bag of popcorn." I'll have to work on that one Tom, as I hadn't been able to successfully sit on anything with Charlotte but the armrest. He also tweaked the VRB by having me introduce a BREAK icon that would allow Charlotte to escape whenever she needed to. Instead of escalating when she didn't want to do an activity, her use of this icon could provide her with a more appropriate behavior. In order to demonstrate the power of the BREAK icon, I would give her an icon of one of her non-preferred activities. Then she could use the BREAK icon in order to avoid escalating. Charlotte caught on quickly. She also realized that the "non-preferred" icon didn't disappear from the VRB. It just delayed her doing that activity.

The VRB was eventually being utilized throughout the day. I'd use it to instruct Charlotte on the day's activities and she'd use it to make requests, choices, and to answer yes or no questions. When it was time for lunch, I would bring out the VRB and ask Charlotte what she wanted. She'd go to the food icons, grab PIZZA, and place it on the VRB's top line. At that point, I would verify her selection by saying, "You want pizza?" She repeated "Pizza" out loud. "Great Charlotte. I love it when you use your words!" Charlotte was beginning to pronounce more and more words after being prompted, and she was not echolalic when doing this. Echolalia, a language disorder found among some people with autism, is just repeating what someone says. Rather than using echolalia, Charlotte would actually initiate spoken language at times.

Charlotte liked to take the classroom trash all the way out to the dumpsters at the rear of the school. This was a closure thing for her. It was good for her to get out of the room, and I'd sometimes suggest that we both make the trip. Prior to using the VRB, Charlotte would just pop up from an activity, gather up a plastic garbage bag, and head out the door. I'd grab a two-way radio and follow her out. After the VRB was instituted, Charlotte would get the TRASH icon and put it on the top line. Great communication Tate! Many times, Charlotte would take the VRB from room to room, knowing it allowed her to communicate.

CHAPTER 11

IN EARLY DECEMBER, I DECIDED to greet Charlotte a little differently when she arrived. I wanted to see if she was really looking at me or was "that guy" just there again? I had taped a small plastic spider on my shoulder. Charlotte got off the bus, climbed the stairs to get into the portable, and immediately gazed at the spider. She tilted her head, then reached out to pick it off my shoulder. After examining it for a moment, she handed it back to me. She did notice something was different! The following day I got a little sillier. I put on a red clown nose that I brought from home. She stared intently, then carefully removed the red nose from my face, smiling all the while. I enjoyed putting a smile on her face in the morning. It kind of set the tone for the day. For the next year or so, I would dawn a different disguise for Charlotte every morning. It could be a hat, mustache, wig, bunny ears, mask, dots glued to my face, feather boas, or a whole host of other get ups. It was part of our daily routine, and Charlotte would begin the day by peering out the bus window to get a view of what that crazy Mr. Dean would look like. The bus drivers even commented that they enjoyed seeing Charlotte's reaction to my daily disguise.

Once inside the classroom, Charlotte would remove her shoes and be barefoot all day. Every now and then she'd go to the grid outside the classroom to "file" her work. Doing this barefoot was okay for most of the year, but winter in Boise, Idaho can be quite cold and snowy.

Charlotte would walk on the cold concrete or on the snow and show no signs of visible discomfort. I started placing her shoes near the door and prompting her to wear them on her excursions. I'd make the "burrrrr" sound, shake my head back and forth, and clasp my arms together. She would mimic the arm position and put on her shoes before going out.

We did lots of Christmas art and craft projects together. She was always excited and followed my directions well. She would even leave a TV program or movie when prompted by my verbal request and reinforced with the velcro request board's ARTS & CRAFTS icon. Because of her necessity for closure, she usually had to finish the movie or program credits before doing anything else, so leaving a movie or show when prompted was a huge advancement.

Charlotte continued to show wonderful improvement in controlling her aggressive behaviors. For the remainder of that winter, there were only a few instances of her getting upset. When she did, I was able to intervene and redirect her. She calmed quickly and held no grudges. She was also able to wait for things. Previously, Charlotte was impulsive and would grab what she needed, even if someone else was using the item. She now demonstrated patience on a daily basis, and her work ethic continued to be strong too. She was doing most of the activities from her work folder whenever she wanted to do them throughout the day. This allowed her to have some control over her daily routine. I didn't care when or where she did the work, as long as it was getting done. I had long ago left my ego outside before entering the classroom. Not trying to control Charlotte's every moment was, itself, a successful intervention.

Sherri, the consulting teacher, had told me earlier that taking baby steps with Charlotte would be the most I could hope for. When I reviewed the first four months of her eighth-grade year, however, I would say we were walking on the moon, taking huge strides. Charlotte had very few major escalations, she was controlling her anger, socializing better with faculty and peers, doing lots of deskwork, following directions well, demonstrating patience, and most important, was communicating appropriately with the VRB as well as initiating spoken language at times. In addition to what she was doing, she wasn't exhibiting a lot of ritualistic behaviors associated with her obsessive-compulsive disorder. Her self-injurious behaviors were also on the decline. I was looking forward to 2005.

Angie wrote an e-mail saying that during the Christmas break, Charlotte wanted to go to school. No amount of discussion could convince her that school was closed. Phil drove her to the school a few times to reinforce that no one was there. Angie was very happy that Charlotte enjoyed school so much. That had not been the case during her seventh grade year. Many times kids come back from a long holiday and it takes a few days to get back into the classroom routine, but Charlotte was ready to go even before the new year came.

After we returned from Christmas break, I designed collages to incorporate reading and math awareness into the curriculum. Charlotte would separate pictures of dogs and cats, then glue them on the space that had the corresponding number of animals. Charlotte could easily demonstrate her reading and counting abilities. For the next project, Charlotte would identify shapes and colors and put them in the proper location on the collage. I brought one of my wife's horse magazines and cut out a variety of pictures. I traced the outline of the picture, then wrote a description of the picture within the outline. Charlotte would read the description, find the correct photo, and glue it on the poster paper. Previously, the completed collages had been filed in the garbage can or outside grid. As she was about to fold, spindle, and mutilate the horse collage, I prompted her to put it in her backpack to show Mom and Dad. She looked at me and agreed! She folded it and placed it in her backpack.

I continued to give Charlotte lots of collages that required her to correctly count, identify colors, and read descriptions. I continually went to the school library to get outdated magazines so I would have a variety of pictures to choose from. I found pictures of animals, jewelry, cars, and other countable items. I really enjoyed our interactions when doing the collage work because they involved communication and patience. I maintained control of the glue so that Charlotte would have to say "Glue please." She was able to remain at a table for extended periods of time, so we were doing four to five collages a day. Most of them actually made it to the backpack when finished. The important thing, in addition to the learning that was taking place, was that Charlotte was having fun. Lessons involving collages would continue to evolve.

Some unexpected teaching moments took place outside the classroom on the sidewalk and curb while Charlotte was waiting for her bus to go home. The bus would normally arrive between 1:50 and 2:00, but for some reason Charlotte would begin waiting any time after 10:30 am. Keeping in mind the major escalation that had occurred at the end of her seventh grade year, I wasn't about to force her to go back into the building. At first, I would just sit with her on the steps or the curb. I would talk to her about anything, such as the weather, stuff happening at my ranch, bugs we saw, and seasons of the year. I'd explained that the bus wouldn't be arriving for a while and we could either do work outside or inside until it came. Sometimes she'd go back inside only to return outside to wait again after a very short time.

One day I brought some chalk with me. I drew a girl's head without any features. Charlotte got the chalk and gave the drawing eyes, ears, nose and a mouth. I wrote "Charl" under the face and she completed "otte". We had watched *Dumbo* earlier in the day and I wrote "Dum" on the sidewalk. She completed "bo" easily. Pretty cool.

During other sidewalk sessions, I would write out 10 to 15 words and then I would verbally spell each word. Charlotte would pronounce each letter after I said it. I would also write part of a word and Charlotte would verbally complete the spelling. She was spelling perfectly. One day I asked her if she wanted to write any words. She got the chalk and wrote, "bus." I responded, "I know Charlotte, you want the bus." I drew a clock and showed her that there was still half an hour until it arrived. She understood and we continued to do more words. I would ask, "More?" and she'd say, "More!" emphatically.

On other days, I brought out flashcards with words for her to write and pronounce. We started with five cards for the day and eventually increased to 20 cards. She was really trying hard to talk. Angie said that Charlotte hadn't been saying many words or writing much since first grade. I wanted to encourage both written and oral forms of communication whenever and wherever possible. Charlotte was slowly coming out of her shell, showing me her abilities.

I had had limited success with YES/NO questions in the past. Now I had a captive audience! I chalked out a big "YES" and "NO" on the sidewalk and proceeded to ask many questions. Most had obvious answers. She would point to her answer and get about 60 per cent correct. I'd mix the questions so there wouldn't be any particular pattern to the answers. I thought she could have done better, but I was just happy that she was participating in the activity.

At other times, we would do math on the sidewalk. I'd draw a bird nest with eggs to count or I'd write out the numbers from one to ten and she would say the numbers with me. Many times I'd stop at a number and she would say the next sequential number by herself! Self initiated spoken language! Great Charlotte.

A wonderful moment occurred one day on the sidewalk. Charlotte had initiated a combination of two syllables repeatedly during the year, "Goo bah." I asked her mom and dad what that meant. They had no idea. I wrote "goo bah" on the sidewalk and said it out loud a few times, then asked Charlotte what it meant. She raised her right arm, waved, and said "Goo bah." "Good bye?" I said. Charlotte continued waving. "Yes, I understand Charlotte!" I jumped up in the air and patted her shoulders. "I understand you, Charlotte. You are communicating!" She was all smiles. I then wrote "go bu" another phrase that she had used repeatedly. I said, "Go bu, go bu. What are you trying to say?" She got the chalk and added an "s" to "bu." "Go bus?" "Go home on the bus?" "Is that it?" Charlotte replied, "Go bu." Again, I excitedly jumped up and down. There was no doubt in her mind that Mr. Dean was a happy guy.

Whenever she was done with chalk work she'd sit on the curb. I'd join her and talk. I'd grab a handful of rocks and we'd count them out loud together as I tossed them into the street. Sometimes she would watch me tie my shoes and then I'd let her practice tying them. She usually wore sandals or boots so she didn't have an opportunity to tie her own shoes.

Another functional (and safety) teaching moment occurred while waiting for the bus. Charlotte would often go into the street when the bus was coming. The bus driver would stop prior to the pickup area for safety reasons. Sometimes Charlotte would return to the curb, and the bus would proceed. Other times she would walk back to where the bus had stopped. I needed to get her to stay on the curb so I drew four footprints on the sidewalk and wrote, "bus" beneath them. I explained that we needed to stand on the footprints while waiting for the bus to drive up. She was cool with that and we had fewer and fewer excursions into the street.

By this time, escalations in the classroom were few and far between. I could tell that undesirable behaviors were just below the surface, but Charlotte was doing a marvelous job of keeping them in check and dealing with anger and frustration with patience. When she did get mad or upset, it only lasted a minute or two and she would calm down quickly.

During this "patience" period, I was able to explain and demonstrate the need to rewind videos. This was viewed earlier as a no-no because it would lead to a video escalation. But now things were different. She'd watch me push the rewind button and wait patiently until the video stopped rewinding. When I pushed eject and the video popped out, she would take it and return it to the video shelf. Charlotte would eventually learn to use a rewinding machine appropriately by herself.

CHAPTER 12

SPRINGTIME IS A TIME FOR growth and blossoming in the world of nature. Charlotte blossomed more than any plant I had ever seen. Her intellect was being challenged and my level of expectations for her work continued to rise.

I challenged her every day with various worksheets. She was appropriately doing addition and subtraction activities. I introduced money concepts and gave her an assortment of money counting worksheets. Time-telling worksheets and a manipulative clock were being utilized daily. She was doing well with identifying full and half-hour increments. With this increase in academic work, there was a corresponding reduction in the non-academic work such as coloring and cut/paste activities.

Charlotte was also showing great growth in the area of communication. I created a yes/no sign that was on a popsicle stick. It had a green side with a YES label and a red side for NO. She began using it frequently in response to questions about lunch. "Do you want your lunch?" YES she showed me. "Do you want pizza?" YES More often than not, she would eat the pizza. Sometimes though, she would whine "A nah!" That meant "no." She'd toss the pizza into the garbage. "What's up? You showed me YES." I'd get her sign and show her the NO side. "Use NO when you don't want food." I guess this was part of her inconsistency thing. On the other hand, I suspected that Miss Tate had a fear of losing control if I knew she could answer YES or NO questions accurately.

Charlotte was also doing activities with the speech and language pathologist (SLP). This was great to see her working with another adult. She would only work sporadically with the aides in our classroom and not at all with Mr. Thomas. She'd usually just blow them off. Charlotte knew the SLP from previous encounters and they always got along well. She even let the SLP sit on her couch while they were working together.

Charlotte's self initiated language continued to improve and increase. Most of the time she would need a prompt like, "What do you say when someone is leaving?" She'd say, "Good bye." She was saying "Thank you," "Good morning," "Scissors," "Cut please," and "Sharpen please" on a regular basis now. On one occasion, she was doing an art project that involved cutting out a character from Winnie the Pooh. She handed me scissors and the characters, which needed some trimming. I tried to get her to speak so I said, "What?" I expect her to say "Cut please." She replied, "Eeyore!" Cool.

Her best vocal accomplishment during that period was to learn to say her teacher's name. I felt that it was important that she be able to identify me. I wrote my name on some tape and put it on my forehead before going to greet her one morning. I pointed to the tape, then to my chest while saying, "Dean." I continued doing that throughout the morning. When we did an art and craft project and she wanted me to cut something, I said, "What's my name?" I repeated my name and Charlotte finally said "Dean-na." Great Tate! From then on, she had great success in saying my name.

I made another sign and hung it around my neck with string. It said, "USE YOUR WORDS." I wore it all day and would hold it up to Charlotte when I wanted a verbal response. I only did this when I knew she had had success in the past with the proper verbal response. This type of prompt worked very well, especially with art and craft projects.

Mr. Thomas and I had a home visit planned with the Tates. I didn't tell Charlotte anything about it, and that day, she rode the bus as usual. We beat the bus to the house and were at the kitchen table when Charlotte entered. She gave us a quizzical look as she walked by. She then proceeded with her after school routine. She put her backpack away, got some chips and an apple, then plopped down to watch some TV. The four adults discussed what she must have been thinking since we were at school when she left, but were at her house when she arrived. I now know exactly what she was thinking, but I have to save that story for later discourse. After her snack, Charlotte came over and did some work with me. Charlotte and I showed her parents how we did a collage and few other art projects. They were happy to see how easily we worked together. The home visit was fun.

During this springtime blossoming, Charlotte did have a few escalations in the classroom. Most of them had to do with videos or the TV. Charlotte wanted to throw videos away after viewing them. We had physical interventions that resulted in visits to the time out room. She'd calm quickly and get an early pardon. After that, I used social stories and a special photo album that had pictures and my pre-recorded, step-by-step instructions on what to do with finished videos. From then on, Charlotte successfully followed those instructions and returned the videos to our video shelf after viewing them.

Another escalation happened when the protective computer furniture arrived one afternoon. Charlotte had been using the computer appropriately for some time and possibly took this computer safety intervention as a slap in the face. Whatever the reason, she was not happy with these new computer stands that protected the monitors. She stayed out of the room while the computers were being transferred to the new stands. Once that was completed, I tried to introduce Charlotte to the new set up. After a cursory inspection, Charlotte began to vocally escalate. Vocal turned to physical pretty quickly. She started pounding on the wood covering. Fortunately, the stands were well made and withstood the barrage. Charlotte's attention then focused on Mr. Thomas and me. She grabbed at our shirts and tried to hit both of us. She was escorted to the time out room and calmed after 10 minutes. While exiting the time out room, she was whining, but was a lot calmer. From then on, she accepted the new furniture addition to our room.

The collage activities evolved tremendously during this period. Instead of just matching pictures with short descriptions, I started using sentences to describe the pictures. There were three to five sentences with space to the right to glue on the corresponding picture. Charlotte would usually start with the top sentence, select the corresponding picture, and then glue it on. I would then say each word of the sentence and Charlotte would repeat each one. She really enjoyed this activity. She would do between four and eleven collages every day! This was allowing her to demonstrate her skills in reading, speaking, and comprehension with one neat little collage. Getting the materials and writing the sentences was keeping me busy. I usually had about 20 collages on reserve. Our school library was purging old magazines one week, and needless to say, I was like a kid in a candy store. *National Geographic, Smithsonian,* and *Sports Illustrated* were all there with pictures and advertisements as well as stories related to animals or teenage themes. Later, the final evolution of the collages would take place.

Mother's Day was approaching and I worked with Charlotte for weeks to prepare a special gift for Angie. I was hoping that Charlotte would say, "Hi Mom" when Angie greeted her at the bus. I used a social story over and over. I would say, "Charlotte goes home on the bus. She gets off the bus and walks up to the front door. Mom opens the door and Charlotte says 'Hi Mom.'" When I got to the "Hi Mom" part, I'd raise my hand to the "hi" position. I would usually go through this entire routine three times in the afternoon and once after Charlotte got on the bus. The bus driver was helpful too, reminding Charlotte just before she got off the bus.

Charlotte would say, "Hi Mom" at the appropriate time when practicing, but didn't have success at home when it counted. Even though Mother's Day came and went without Charlotte delivering "the gift," I was undaunted. She was so close to spontaneously greeting her mother. We continued working on the social story. Two weeks after Mother's Day, Charlotte came through. She said "Hi Mom" when she got home. Angie was thrilled. She wrote a nice e-mail stating what had happened. The e-mail was forwarded to the special education area supervisor, who added some information about the various accommodations that had been made for Charlotte and how they had helped. The supervisor then sent the amended e-mail to the district quadrant director. Thanks Charlotte!

The spring months were fabulous for Charlotte. Escalations and behavior problems were less in severity and duration. Her work ethic hit all time heights. A typical April day's output looked like this: completing nine sentence collages, four toilet roll art projects, two paper plate art projects, two cut and paste activities, some clock worksheets with manipulatives, money and addition worksheets, some YES/NO questions, reading and pronouncing ten to fifteen flashcards, and doing a word writing activity. She had come a long way by the end of her eighth-grade year.

CHAPTER 13

DURING SUMMER SCHOOL, THE GOAL is generally to have students maintain the skills they obtained during the regular school year. With Charlotte, it was easy to continue with the various academic activities she had been doing.

Kelly was a student teacher working in our summer school program. She was to start a program for elementary kids with autism the following year and could get good experience by working in our classroom. She was initially a little tentative around Charlotte. I assured her that Charlotte had not hit a female at all during the school year. I encouraged her to start slowly and do things that Charlotte was familiar with. She was successful in doing some collages and later they would "buddy read" together. Charlotte was generalizing her skills with another adult and it was neat for me to see "my" student working with another teacher.

One day Kelly asked me if I thought Charlotte would like her fingernails painted. Charlotte didn't usually like anything on her skin, but maybe fingernails would be OK. We both talked to her about how teenage girls enjoyed painting their nails. She was listening and showed much interest in doing this age-appropriate activity. Charlotte selected the color and Kelly painted her nails. At first, Miss Tate thought it was pretty cool, but after a few minutes, she decided to remove the foreign substance. She went to the sink and washed off most of the polish. Then she accepted Kelly's help to remove the rest with nail polish remover.

Throughout the school year, Charlotte would only leave the room during school hours to go inside the main building or to go to the garbage bins. We never went on walks with the other students. But one day during summer school, Phil brought in a tandem bike for the students to use. Charlotte had ridden with Phil many times and she decided to allow me into this favorite activity. Whenever we rode around the empty parking lot, she was all smiles. She made her happy sounds when we went over the speed bumps. It was great to get Charlotte outside the classroom.

Charlotte started using the computer more often and for longer periods of time than during the regular school year. She tried new games after watching other students demonstrate them. She especially liked a coloring program that allowed her to color various pictures on the screen. I found it interesting that about 80 percent of the time, she selected only one color to fill in all the parts of the picture. However, some pictures had the option of coloring by numbers. On those, Charlotte would check the number and use the corresponding colors to fill in the pictures. These pictures would come out looking great. I'm not sure why she colored with only one color on so many of the others.

Charlotte also enjoyed a computer program called Wordwise. This program would show a picture and give three descriptive words to choose from. Charlotte would choose the correct word almost every time. The first time she did the program, she flew through 98 problems. She then repeated the same effort. I asked her if she wanted more. "More" she replied immediately. I changed the subject matter and she clicked and answered 100 more questions. For the most, part Charlotte had successful behavior while using the computer, and she was compliant with my requests to transition from the computer to a new activity. This was a very positive thing for her to leave a preferred activity. However, there were a few escalations during the six weeks of summer school resulting from computer work or TV disputes. Charlotte got upset when the computer froze up, but calmed quickly when I intervened and suggested that a visit to the time out room might be in her future. Another escalation was when she wanted the TV off in the other room. Another student wanted it on, and I agreed with the other student. Charlotte did not agree. She came at me swinging and ended up visiting the time out room for a brief period of time. Upon exiting calmly, she went to the TV and turned it off. I turned it back on and after some paddy cake grabbing at my hands, I escorted her to the time out room again. She calmed and exited again. Déjà vu was about to happen. She again turned the TV off. I turned it on and we paddy caked again. After her third visit to the time out room, I asked Charlotte to apologize to me. After prompting, she said, "I sorry Dean-na."

The last escalation episode of the summer had to do with work refusal. I showed Charlotte the VRB with a clock icon and then a video icon on the top line. Charlotte took the VRB and returned it to the shelf in the other room. I retrieved it and prompted her to start the clock worksheet. Again she returned the board to the other room. I brought it back in and showed her the order of activities that I expected. She grabbed and squeezed my hands and fingers. I let her do that while saying, "No hit" and "Stop." She ended up going to the time out room for a brief 45-second stay. Upon exiting, she did the clock worksheet without protesting.

Summer school ended on a positive note. Charlotte had some chips and I went over to sit with her. I assumed she'd "toe" me off the couch but she didn't. I asked her for a chip and she offered me the bag. I took a few chips and ate them. I was satisfied and left the couch for a nearby chair. A few minutes later, Charlotte came over to me and offered me more chips! She ended up feeding them to me one by one and watched intently as I chewed each one.

The whole class had a barbecue to celebrate the end of summer school. Charlotte joined everyone outside, but was very anxious to return to the classroom. Whenever she started toward the door, I verbally requested her to stay with us outside, and she complied each time. She not only stayed outside, but with lots of prompting, Charlotte even tried to play croquet! Angie and Phil were there and looked pleased that Charlotte was joining her peers and socializing. All and all, Charlotte had a fantastic eighth-grade year at school.

CHAPTER 14

THERE WAS ABOUT SIX WEEKS between the end of summer school and the beginning of the new school session. I thought it was important for Charlotte to know that I had not disappeared, so I invited the Tates to my ranch during that time. Upon arrival, Charlotte got out of the car just before it came to a complete stop. She was very excited to be at my house.

On the two previous classroom field trips to my ranch, Charlotte had been drawn to my family's video collection. This visit would be no different. She parked herself by the shelves and made a selection. As she was watching her movie choice, Phil and I discussed the previous year's accomplishments and the improvement in Charlotte's behavior both at home and at school. Phil said that both he and Angie were very pleased about Charlotte having her best school year ever. And Charlotte was a happy kid at home also. She was not so rigid with her rules and routines. She could leave activities when prompted without any escalation.

I asked Charlotte to help me collect chicken eggs. She immediately left the TV to do the gathering. She got six eggs and helped me wash the shells. We packed them in a carton for a safe trip home. I found out later that she had Angie fry them one by one and Charlotte chowed down the entire half dozen eggs!

Charlotte's ninth grade school year could be divided into two parts. From August to January was amazing, and February to the end of the school year was almost unbelievable.

Charlotte's behavior continued to improve at school. She was socializing with the other students better than ever. She was willing to let anyone share her couch. If the couch were full, Charlotte would sit in a reclining chair. There was no rigid adherence to sitting in any special location. She also was patient with the other students when they changed TV stations or put in their videos. She could now rewind a movie by herself and put it away. Whenever school was over for the day, Charlotte would turn off the TV and get on the bus with minimal prompting and little, if any resistance.

Charlotte was more receptive to going for walks around the school than she had been in the past. After three abortive attempts, she eventually walked up to the tennis courts with me. Another student had brought in a three wheel recombinant bike (a tricycle looking bike for big folks). Charlotte loved to peddle it, but she lacked steering experience. I ran along the side of her to help in that endeavor. Charlotte was all smiles, making her happy noises throughout the experience.

During October, I noticed that Charlotte was exhibiting some ritualistic behaviors. She was grounding herself more often and had a compulsion for moving the couch out from the wall, walking around it, then pushing it back to the wall. She could even accomplish this effort with Andy remaining on the couch for the ride. A gouge in the wall was developing due to the couch being moved and hitting the wall so often. A work order solved that issue by having a wood plank placed on the wall for protection.

There was another ritualistic behavior that Charlotte would exhibit. She would be walking in a straight line, perform a perfect pirouette, and continue on. She was in a dance class after school so I attributed this latest compulsion to practicing her dance moves.

Charlotte surprised me one day when there was a scheduled fire drill. During prior drills, I would pre-teach what was going to happen, hoping that she would join the rest of the class in the gathering area. We never made it out of the room. We had special dispensation from the principals to remain in the room. I promised that if there were a real fire, I would get her out safely. Charlotte would focus on the flashing light of the classroom alarm. The loud noise bugged me more than it did her. However, this day when the alarm went off, Miss Tate got her shoes, walked out with me, and joined her classmates. She was looking at all the students gathered in their assigned areas. She waited patiently until the release bell sounded and then walked back to the room.

One of the goals on Charlotte's Individual Education Plan (IEP) was to wash her hands after using the bathroom and before eating lunch. Her folks said that she washed them appropriately at home, but I had had no success with her at school. It was an important functional skill that she needed to master. At first, I tried to prompt her to just put her right hand under the running water. She continually hesitated. Finally I got the VRB and placed a WASH HANDS icon along with the MOVIE icon. I verbalized what I wanted her to do. She really wanted the movie so she finally zoomed her hand through the water. She got her movie. The next time I prompted her, I required her to keep her hand under the water a little longer. She complied without resistance. I applied soap the next time and she immediately went to the running water to wash it off. Ah ha! She didn't like the tactile stimulation of the soap. After gaining that valuable knowledge, I was able to use that aversion to soap to get her to wash up at any time.

I bought Charlotte a pink T-shirt for a Christmas present, but was not sure if she would even wear it, as she was pretty particular about what she wore. Sometimes she chose to wear the same clothes each day for an entire week. This kept Angie busy washing the clothes at night after Charlotte was asleep and having them ready for her to wear the next day. To my surprise, Miss Tate wore my gift the day after I gave it to her and would wear it even more after we returned from Christmas break.

Charlotte's escalations during the first five months were few. Most of them had to do with the television and one occurred with the computer. In some instances, I was able to verbally intervene and reduce the magnitude of her frustration or anger. The other times, Charlotte was escorted to the time out room where she cooled off quickly and rejoined the classroom. The computer escalation was a great example of how far Charlotte had come in dealing with her frustration. She had been getting vocally loud and had hit the keyboard with her fist. I immediately went to her and asked what was wrong. She grabbed my hands and fingers, squeezing them hard. I stood my ground and calmly asked if I could help. She reached up and got a handful of my shirt. I told her not to rip my shirt. I asked her if she wanted Disney, Aladdin, or Little Mermaid, but to no avail. I had the white board with me and showed it to her, "Use the board and tell me what you want!" She ignored my request. I continued, saying "Charlotte, use your words!" She finally said, "Do pee." I wrote it on the white board and repeated it a few times. "Do pee, Do pee, Dopey. Do you want Dopey?" She smiled and was quiet. I was pretty sure I guessed correctly. I typed Dopey in the search engine and a herd of Dopeys and his six buddies appeared. She settled in to scrutinize all of the pictures. I verbally reinforced that she had the power of communication. "Use your words!" would become a familiar phrase coming out of my mouth.

Charlotte's academic output exploded during this period. She was doing all the previous activities in addition to everything else I introduced.

There was little, if any resistance to new material. In fact, she exhibited enthusiasm and curiosity toward all the work activities. One of the new efforts she engaged in was the Read Naturally program. It consisted of short stories with comprehension questions. We'd "buddy read" the story, then Charlotte would select the correct answer from three choices for each question. It was great to see her circling answers. This skill could come in handy in the future.

Charlotte found some of our activities to be very enjoyable. I introduced her to tic tac toe. This was a good way to foster patience in the form of turn taking. She understood after a few trials and enjoyed playing a couple of games each day. Another activity was a matching game using sounds from a tape player and pictures on various cards. She had played this game two years earlier. One day she found the game on a shelf and grabbed my hand to lead me into the other side of the portable. I set up the four different bingo like cards that had nine pictures on each card. I played the tape recorder, and the first sound was heard. Charlotte went right to the correct card, found the image, and placed a token on it. She repeated this for the second sound. She seemed to quickly know what card had the picture represented by each sound. Her memory of which pictures were on each card was pretty impressive after a two-year hiatus.

Charlotte's communication efforts were the highlight of the first half of that year. Some of her oral language was prompted. "What do you say when someone gives you something?" "Thank you" she'd say. "What do you say when someone is leaving?" "Goodbye" was her reply. I'd often let her know how happy I was to hear her voice. "Charlotte, I love to hear your words!" Other language was spontaneous. She said, "Go away" when I sat down on her couch with a magazine. She would tell another student, "Go please" or "Move please" when they stood in front of the TV. She'd greet me with a "Good morning" upon arrival. She also continued to use previously spoken words like, "Cut please", "Sharpen", "Scissors", "Movie", and my favorite, "Dean-na." Charlotte also continued to try very hard to pronounce words on flashcards. Once again, she said some things spontaneously and others after I gave her the first syllable as a hint. Still others needed to be pronounced completely by me prior to her saying the word.

After a while, she started writing more. While making collages one day, I drew a line under each descriptive sentence. After Charlotte placed the correct picture with the first sentence, she picked up a marker and rewrote the entire sentence on the line. She then repeated each word after I said it. I would incorporate this final "evolution" of the collage for all future efforts. Thanks for the improvement, Miss Tate!

I carried a portable white board from room to room. Whenever Charlotte wanted something, I encouraged her to write it out. She had some success in doing this. She wrote PIZZA or MOVIE on occasion. At other times, I would write out a question and give two or three choices for answers. Charlotte would then circle the correct answer.

The last communication device Charlotte showed improvement with was the alphabet board. It has the 26 letters, numbers one through ten, and YES / NO printed on a laminated paper. In the beginning of the school year, I geared the lessons for success. Before long, Charlotte could finger-touch letters that made single words. She progressed to touching out two word answers along with appropriate YES/NO responses. "What do you go home on?" A BUS she typed out. "Where do you want to go on the Internet?" DISNEY was her response. One day, she wanted a certain computer game. She typed out CH, then stopped. I guessed "Chipmunk Coloring?" She pointed to YES on the alpha board. "Great Charlotte, we are communicating!" We played an animal sound game with the alpha board. "What makes this sound......moo?" COW she typed. She correctly typed out DOG and CAT after hearing their sounds. Angie also reported some success at home. Charlotte had wanted to go somewhere so Angie gave her an alpha board. Charlotte typed out ALBERTSONS, a nearby grocery store. This generalization to home was a great thing to hear about.

CHAPTER 15

IN DECEMBER OF 2005, THE Tates asked me if I would be interested in going with Phil and Charlotte to Austin, Texas to an autism clinic. It featured a teaching program called Rapid Prompting Method (RPM). RPM was developed by Soma Mukhopadhyay, the mother of Tito, the boy who wrote the book, The Mind Tree. This was one of the books I had read during the summer after I had met Charlotte. RPM is a method used to teach academics, but communication is also enhanced with the process. It is designed to activate the reasoning part of the brain. RPM elicits maximum output from the student by giving rapid verbal, auditory, visual, and tactile prompts in order to access the open learning channel. This method presumes competence in receptive language comprehension that is at or near age/grade level. The Tates figured that if Charlotte was going to be successful with this method, then it would have to be utilized both at home and at school. I enthusiastically accepted their offer of going to Austin and read up on the program. The Tates provided me with a DVD about the method and I was excited to learn another teaching technique that might help my student.

The DVD showed numerous examples of Soma working with a variety of students with autism. It was fascinating to watch her get responses out of kids who were in constant physical motion and with eyes continuously darting from place to place. It was difficult for me to watch Soma working with one of the students. Claire was loud, nonverbal, aggressive, and reminded me of the "old" Charlotte. Initially, she was pretty combative with Soma. Keep in mind that Soma is a very petite Indian lady. This student was constantly trying to hit and slap at her. Claire would rip up the paper, throw the pencil, and was totally non-cooperative. Her behaviors did not deter Soma one bit. Soma continued to work with her and after the third day of teaching, Claire's misbehaviors had subsided and she was making appropriate choices. It was apparent that she was learning.

As the trip date neared, I learned from Mr. Thomas that my going to the clinic was not a sure thing. I had told Mr. Thomas about the trip the day after the Tates had asked me to go, but I had taken no other action. Mr. Thomas said that the Tates had not gone through the proper channels to inform the district or his supervisor about the trip. I was quite disappointed. The district would be getting the benefit of having one of their employees learn a teaching technique that might help not only Charlotte, but future students as well. It wouldn't cost the district a penny, as the Tates were willing to pay for my airfare, the hotel, food, and my fee for observing at the clinic. The Tates had wanted me to go because I was the one teaching Charlotte at school. The program would be far less effective if it was only used at home by the Tates.

The district had decided to send Mr. Thomas and a district psychologist to Austin to evaluate the RPM method. However, a week before the trip, Mr. Thomas told me that I could also go, but only if I used my personal days. In other words, the district would not pay my salary for the time that I'd be gone. It was highly unusual for the district to approve travel for non certified employees, but I felt that this was an unusual case as the Tates were paying my expenses, and the district would benefit from my going. I checked my balance of personal days, found that I had enough, so I told Mr. Thomas that I would, indeed, be going on my own time. Within a few days, my supervisor showed up in our classroom. She informed me that even though there were payroll concerns as well as approvals needed, the district had decided to pay my salary after all. I appreciated their decision even though I would have used my personal days in a heartbeat. Anything to help my student.

In the days leading up to the trip, I had been pre-teaching about the adventure to Charlotte. We looked at a map of the United States and plotted our trip. Boise to Denver, then Denver to Austin. We discussed the direction that our flight would be going and how long each trip segment would take. Charlotte seemed to grasp all of the information. Phil said that Charlotte had been on planes before and had done well.

After watching the Soma DVD, I tried to replicate some of her work with Charlotte prior to our trip. She had been doing well with the alpha board and with making choices for answers to questions. These skills would definitely come in handy when working with Soma.

My family met up with Phil and Charlotte at the airport on Sunday. We exchanged pleasantries and I said goodbye to my wife and two kids. When we were going through security, Charlotte was doing her pirouettes and grounding maneuvers. She seemed excited to be going on a trip. Charlotte did wonderfully on the flight to Denver. Phil brought a portable DVD player with lots of movies. Charlotte was content watching movies throughout the flight. I felt uncomfortable with the looks Charlotte got from people when she made her noises or flapped her hand in the air. She would often do these things during a favorite part in the movie. Phil was accustomed to the onlookers, but it was a new experience for me. I was use to Charlotte's behaviors in the classroom, but not out in public. I got a small inkling of what it was like to have a child with autism.

We arrived in Denver and had an hour to kill during our layover. Phil walked around with Charlotte and bought her some popcorn. Phil was always so calm with Charlotte. He talked to her a lot and Charlotte would look to him for assurance and direction by tilting her head slightly while looking directly at him. Phil seemed to know what Charlotte wanted. The next leg of the trip to Austin also went just fine. It turned out that Charlotte was a very good traveler.

CHAPTER 16

THE MORNING AFTER OUR ARRIVAL, Phil, Charlotte, and I met Mr. Thomas and the district psychologist at the autism clinic. It was called HALO for Helping Autism through Learning and Outreach. Soma greeted us and was all business. She immediately escorted us upstairs. There were two rooms. One was for the instructional process and the other for observation. The observation room had a big table and a TV feed from the video camera in the instructional room. Phil, Charlotte, and I followed Soma into the instructional room, while Mr. Thomas and the district psychologist went to the observation room.

Soma got right to it, trying to evaluate Charlotte's learning style. She started with number sequences. Charlotte was paying attention, but then suddenly grabbed at the pieces of paper that Soma was using. Phil and I were braced for an escalation and a possible physical intervention. Soma, with her East Indian accent, proclaimed, "Oh, we are grabbing the paper!" She immediately tore another piece of paper, wrote GRABBING on it, and taped it onto Charlotte's forearm. This was to be a distracter for her behavior. I looked at Phil and smiled. "No way will she allow that to stay on her arm." To my amazement, she did leave it on, and Soma continued the lesson. Charlotte would touch the paper, but didn't remove it. Soma had Charlotte answer questions about statements. For example, Soma said, "A doctor works in a hospital." Then she wrote that sentence down on a blank piece of paper. Soma wrote HOSPITAL and SCHOOL on two small pieces of paper. "Did I say, 'A doctor works in a hospital' or did I say, 'A doctor works in a school'?" She presented the two choices to Charlotte. Charlotte circled the word HOSPITAL. Soma then had Charlotte trace the letters in "hospital" on a stencil. After that, she had Charlotte tape the small piece of paper with a circled HOSPITAL onto the larger paper with the previously written sentence. She then repeated the process with a new statement. The questions posed during this first encounter were geared to enable Charlotte to have success. And she did. Charlotte was nailing each answer. After a while, Soma created a triangle shaped paper and wrote the word GOOD on it. She removed the GRABBING paper and replaced it with the GOOD one. "You have not been grabbing so I will give you a GOOD triangle." Charlotte seemed proud to wear this new commendation.

Charlotte was very curious about the red dot that was on Soma's forehead. Her curiosity was becoming a distraction to the session, so Soma stopped and discussed her dot. After that discussion, the dot lost its mystique as a distracter, although Charlotte still checked it out on occasion.

I was impressed with two things that had gone on. First, the pace of the lesson was very fast. When Soma sensed a lack of focus, she would change the topic. This kept Charlotte's interest. When Charlotte tossed a pencil, Soma created a FIDGETING paper, taped it to her arm, and continued the lesson. Second, I couldn't believe that Charlotte had remained seated for the entire 45-minute session. She had sat with me at a table doing collages and crafts for 10 to 15 minutes at a time. When it came to academics, however, five minutes was the most I could hope for.

Phil and I both enjoyed seeing Charlotte have this success. Phil and Angie had spent thousands of dollars and traveled around the country trying to find someone or some program that could help Charlotte. It certainly appeared that HALO was providing more bang for the buck than any of the other high priced programs.

After the first session, Phil and I met outside with Mr. Thomas and the psychologist to discuss what had transpired. We could barely contain our enthusiasm, but it was evident that Mr. Thomas was skeptical. He thought Soma was placing the pieces of paper in a certain way so that Charlotte would pick the correct answer. Phil and I countered his assessment by saying that Soma had varied the placement of the correct answers on the right and left sides with no apparent pattern. Mr. Thomas was not persuaded. I thought that if he and the psychologist were in the instructional room for a future session while Phil and I watched from the video room, that they might get a better feel for Charlotte's performance.

Phil, Charlotte, and I went to lunch. On the way, I asked Charlotte how hard she felt the first session was. I gave her two choices, HARD and EASY. She circled EASY. Phil called Angie and described the first session. Our car was buzzing with excitement.

The topic for the afternoon session was history. Soma started talking about the pilgrims, religious freedom, England, the Mayflower, and the journey to the New World. When Soma began the lesson, I thought to myself that the subject matter was way over Charlotte's head. Phil and I continually exchanged glances of astonishment as Charlotte chose the correct answers to Soma's queries. In addition to circling answers on paper and tracing in the stencil, Charlotte was using an alpha board to finger type out the correct answers. The pace was furious and held Charlotte's attention. Later, when I asked Charlotte to evaluate that session, she circled HARD.

That evening, the three of us took a swim at the hotel's pool. I was surprised at how well Charlotte could swim. Phil said she had lots of practice at home in the Tates' pool and also while boating. Later that night, Mr. Thomas and the psychologist joined us for a birthday party for Charlotte. We sang "Happy Birthday" and Charlotte enjoyed the company. All of us enjoyed the birthday cake. Phil and I couldn't stop talking about how much Soma got out of Charlotte. We were looking forward to the next day's sessions.

The first session on the following day started with lots of math. Charlotte was doing well, focusing on the lesson and behaving appropriately. She was still interested in Soma's red dot, but it was not too distracting. Soma switched to talking about rain. "What comes to mind when I say rain?" Charlotte typed out on an alpha board, WET, CLOUD. Then Soma went on to explain about the water cycle, asked questions, and all the while prompting Charlotte to type out the answers. Charlotte again described this session as HARD. She was a real trooper, though, demonstrating once more that she could sit at a table, behave, and do academics for 45 minutes.

Soma began the afternoon session by reviewing the water cycle. Next it was time to elaborate on words by typing associated words. Soma said, "Dog" and Charlotte typed PET. Next she asked about, "House." Charlotte typed ROOMS. "Tree." Charlotte typed LEAF. "What comes to mind when I say sun?" DAY was typed. When Charlotte didn't respond to "Yawn," Soma quickly changed the subject to sequential math numbers. She was using three- digit examples and Charlotte was hanging in there. I had previously discussed only the numbers one through 20 with her at school. After a while, Soma returned to "yawn." Charlotte typed TIRED. Next was a letter-writing exercise. "Do you start a letter with 'The sky is blue' or 'Dear Mom'?" She wrote the choices down on two pieces of paper. Charlotte circled "Dear Mom." The letter was pertaining to our trip. Soma continued, "I am in Austin" or "A cat is an animal." Charlotte continued to circle the correct answers and then taped each one onto a blank paper in the appropriate places for a letter format. When the letter was done, the conversation turned to how to get the letter to Mom. "Would you drop it in a letterbox or the trash?" "Does the mailman work in a post office or a restaurant?" Charlotte continued to circle, and then spell the correct answers. There was no observable "smoke and mirrors" as Mr. Thomas had suggested. His skepticism and pessimism, however, were unwavering. Phil and I chose to believe our eyes and were very impressed with Soma's system for teaching. When I thought back to conversations I had with Mr. Thomas prior to the trip, I could remember hearing only pessimism from him, such as, "There is no magic bullet to cure autism." "I didn't even finish watching the Soma DVD. It was too boring and hard to watch." This adversarial approach from him wouldn't change.

Soma asked Charlotte to talk about her birthday party. LOVED IT was her typed response. "What part did you like the best?" EATING. "What kind of presents would you like to get?" IPOD CDS. An IPOD and CD's, wow, we never really knew Charlotte. Phil and I just shook our heads in amazement. The lesson was then switched to doing lots of addition problems. At the end of that day's session, Soma told a story. She asked questions about the content of the story and Charlotte would type the answers on the alpha board. Great job Charlotte.

That afternoon, the three of us went to a nearby underground cave outside of Austin. We had the tour guide all to ourselves. A train took us into the opening of the cave, and Charlotte was all smiles. We saw lots of beautiful formations, including stalactites and stalagmites. Each segment of the cave had its own set of lights, so we would get to a dark area and wait for the guide to find the light switch. That is, Phil and I waited for the lights. Charlotte marched on ahead through the darkness like a real spelunker. We were surprised to see how far she had ventured in the dark, sometimes up to 50 feet. She was quite the brave explorer.

On the last day, the sessions focused on word association, math, identifying nouns in sentences, reviewing the water cycle, and talking about pollution. Charlotte was asked, "What comes to mind when you think of weather?" She typed out SNOW, WIND, then HURRICANE. Phil and I were blown away. Hurricane? Where did that come from? Wait a second, Hurricane Katrina had happened about five months earlier. Charlotte must have absorbed what she saw or heard on the news. Wow, that was pretty impressive.

At the end of the final session, Phil and I tried using the Rapid Prompting Method (RPM) method with Charlotte. Phil struggled when presenting the choices. I had practiced the night before, so was much more prepared than Dad. I presented Charlotte with information on our solar system. She was interested and correctly chose the right answers to my questions. She taped the answers onto a blank paper after I wrote out the questions. Although it went pretty well, I was a babe in the woods compared to Soma. She can really think on her feet and has a ton of experience working with kids who have autism.

We were able to do a little sight seeing in Austin on the last day. We went to Texas University and toured their museum. Charlotte really enjoyed the dinosaur area. She was interested in all the exhibits. We stopped by the gift shop and picked up some souvenirs. The flight home was uneventful. It felt good to be back home, and I looked forward to continuing using the RPM technique with Charlotte in the classroom setting. Soma recommended starting off with second and third grade curriculum in order to establish success, and then add some age appropriate materials. She thought Charlotte would zoom through the first part and quickly be working at grade level. She said that we should include current events, word association, and ask questions after reading books to Charlotte.

Charlotte Tate

Charlotte with her parents, Phil and Angie

Charlotte and Dean working with flashcards

Charlotte and Dean working with flashcards

Charlotte and Dean practicing writing

"Gimme five"

Riding tandem with Dad

Charlotte and Dean

Dean's family Armida, Tess, and Chas

CHAPTER 17

IN ORDER TO REPLICATE SOMA'S work area in our classroom, Mr. Thomas thought it would be best for Charlotte and I to work in the time out room. There would be fewer distractions in there. I was concerned that the time out room might be construed as a negative place for Charlotte. Previously, that was the place where she ended up when her behavior was unacceptable. But I gave it a try. I brought in a table and two chairs. There were two walls where we could display her completed work. I showed Charlotte the file folder of Soma-type work. It was labeled RED DOT WORK. I wanted her to know that whenever I brought out this folder, our work would take place in the time out room.

I started by discussing the three forms of water: liquid, solid, and gas. I presented questions about each of the forms. Charlotte would choose the correct answer from two pieces of paper and tape it to the corresponding question. She did great in answering the questions and proudly taped the completed sheet onto the wall. Then she bolted from the room and started watching TV. Our first Red Dot work had gone well except for Charlotte wanting to leave so quickly. Later that day, Charlotte did a variety of other academic activities with great success.

The following day was much the same. With prompting, Charlotte would turn off the TV and complete Red Dot work in the time out room with me. Our Red Dot sessions were lasting about 20 minutes each, which was considerably longer than the previous five-minute work sessions we had had. My anxiety about working in the time-out room proved to be unfounded.

On subsequent days, we discussed Columbus and his journey to the New World, the water cycle (she was able to correctly label the various stages on a worksheet with diagrams), King Tut, volcanoes, and the rainforest. In each session, I would present the material and question Charlotte. She would tape the chosen answers onto a piece of paper and then tape the whole sheet to the wall. She was really enjoying learning about new things. Her ability to turn off the TV when prompted was a huge positive development. One day I told her I was going to the bathroom and that when I came back, she would have to turn off the TV and do Red Dot work. When I emerged from the bathroom, the TV was off and Charlotte was patiently waiting for me at the desk in the time out room. Wow!

When we did flashcard word association activities during Red Dot sessions, Charlotte had fun, and I gained insightful information about her. I would show her a flashcard and ask her what comes to mind? Two cards elicited remarkable responses. When I presented a flashcard for a cave and asked what she thought about, she typed STALAGMITES. "What flies in a cave?" BAT "What did we ride on to go down to the cave in Texas?" TRAIN "What liquid did we see in the cave?" WATER Nice job Charlotte.

Another flashcard showed a person sleeping with a thought bubble. "What is this?" DREAM "Do you dream?" YES "What do you dream about?" A REAL FRIEND "What kind of friend?" A BOYFRIEND I teared up a little. "Maybe someday, Charlotte. If you continue communicating and behaving like you are, you could have a boyfriend."

In addition to doing Red Dot work and regular classroom work, I introduced "Free Thinking Questions." I prepared questions that would help me understand Charlotte's autism and also allow her to express her feelings. Charlotte would type out the answers and I would write her responses on paper. The following conversations happened throughout a period of a couple of weeks.

"How do you feel today?" GOOD

"Have you heard of autism?" YES

"Do you have autism?" YES

"What is autism?" SICK ON BRAIN

I told her that Autism took various forms in different people. "It affects the speech and language parts of your brain. You are now communicating and doing great! You are working really hard! What else do you want to say?" PRAISE WOW

"Do you like praise?" YES

"Do I give you enough praise?" YES

Later that afternoon she was flapping in front of the TV while the credits were rolling.

"Do you read all the words?" NO

"Why do you flap when the credits roll?" PEACE

"It brings peace to your brain?" YES

"Why do you ground yourself?" TO RELAX

She then gagged herself by putting her fingers down her throat. She had done this previously, usually after saying words or making noises. I was hoping to get some profound answer when I asked, "Why do you gag yourself?" NO REASON was her typed response. Darn, no insight there. I continued my query.

"Do you want people to treat you like a little girl or a big girl?" BIG

"What do you want to search for on Google?" TEENAGER STUFF

Later that day we had completed some Red Dot work and Charlotte was quickly departing the room for the TV. "Do you have any questions for me?" She was halfway out the door and stopped in her tracks. She came back and typed out… ONLY WHY PEOPLE THINK I AM STUPID   After 16 years of limited communication, her first question had to do with self-esteem. I had told Charlotte that I would always tell her the truth. I believe that my commitment to her helped her to trust me and to break down some of her barriers. That commitment was now being put to the test. I didn't want to hurt her feelings, but I also wouldn't violate the trust that had developed between us. I explained that people don't understand autism and some of the rituals that she did were kind of weird. I told her that she was smart, not stupid, and that "People will know you are smart if you can communicate better. Any other questions?" WHY DO PEOPLE LOOK AT ME   I told her two reasons. "Because you flap your hands and ground yourself and people are curious. When you aren't doing the autistic stuff, they are looking at you because you are a very pretty girl." Charlotte accepted my answers and left the room.

On subsequent days, I continued to focus on her communication and hammered away with more "Free Thinking Questions."

"Why don't you like to go into the school building?" BECAUSE NOBODY REACHES OUT AND LEARNS ABOUT AUTISM

"Why do you like working with me?" BECAUSE YOU ARE NICER AND LIKE ME

"How do you feel today?" TREMENDOUS

"Because you are communicating?" YES

"Where would you like to go on vacation?" BEACH

"A beach on a lake or the ocean?" OCEAN   I shared this tidbit with Phil and Angie.

"What happens in your brain when you try to talk?" TROUBLE PRONOUNCING WORDS

"Why are you so pretty?" NOSE   BLUE EYES   We had a nice laugh when I questioned her about her pretty nose.

"What activities do you like best?" TO WALK ON THE RIVER (Not like Jesus. We have a beautiful walkway along the Boise River.)

"What is your favorite movie?" BEAUTY AND THE BEAST

"What movie would you like to see?" SNOW DOGS

"What do you know about Iraq?" WAR VERY HOT (In Texas, Charlotte had mentioned Iraq for an answer to the Soma question, "What worries you?")

"What comes to mind when you think of God?" PRAY TO GOD

"Do you pray to God?" NO

"If you did, what would you pray for?" TALK TO PEOPLE

I asked her if she had any statements or questions for me.

WHAT PEOPLE SAY OUTSIDE CAN BE VERY MEAN

"I know, they just don't understand autism?"

WHY DO PEOPLE ORDER ME AROUND

"Who orders you around?" STUPID PEOPLE

"Because they don't know you are really smart."

WHY DO KIDS PRETEND TO FEAR ME

"They aren't pretending. They remember some of the things you did inside the school building. Do you want kids to think you are nice or mean?" NICE

"Why do you like little kids' shows on TV and in movies?" THEY ARE REALLY FUNNY LOOKING

"Why do you make your noises?" I DO IT BECAUSE IT FEELS GOOD

"Do I talk too fast for you?" NO

"Do you understand every word I say to you?" YES

Charlotte had been exhibiting seizure like symptoms. She would stop and tilt her head. It looked like she was deep in thought and her eyelids would flutter a little. I inquired....

"What is happening in you brain when you stop and think?" I HAVE NO IDEA

"Do you see lights or flashes?" NO

I informed the school nurse and she came over with some information about seizures. Mr. Thomas also alerted Charlotte's folks. I started keeping a tally when I observed the activity.

I continued with the Free Thinking Questions.

"How do you feel today?" DELIGHTFUL

"Would you like to meet a teenage girl from the building?" YES "I'll set it up."

"What are some things you are good at?" SPELLING WORDS WALKING READING BOOKS

"What things confuse you?" WHAT PEOPLE SAY ABOUT AUTISTIC PEOPLE

"What do they say?" THAT WE ARE STUPID AND UNTEACHABLE

"I don't think they know what they are talking about. You are smart and I will teach you."

"What do you like best about your house?" THE TELEVISION

"Do you know what self-esteem is?" YES

"Do you have low or high self esteem?" LOW

"You should be feeling better and better now that you are communicating." YES

"What things stress you out?" SOMETHING LIKE THE WORLD WAR IN IRAQ

"Why do you color a picture nicely, then color over the whole picture when you are done?" BECAUSE I WANT TO REMOVE THE PICTURE FROM ON THE PAPER

"Why do you sometimes pull back or rub off where I touch you on the arm or hand?" IT FEELS UNCLEAN

The next question Charlotte asked was not only her longest to date, it was also perplexing.

WHY DO PEOPLE LOOK AT WOMEN WHO WEAR RED SHIRTS ON THEIR BODIES AND LOOK LIKE PROSTITUTES

This question completely caught me off guard. Wow, what prompted this question? She knew the difference between "looking like" a prostitute and being one. This question also reaffirmed to me that Charlotte had a higher intellect than any of the experts had ever dreamed she had. After I recomposed myself, I answered her. "Because their clothes are too tight and it shows off their bodies too much." I forwarded her question to Angie and Phil, hoping that they might shed some light on the incident that prompted her question. They couldn't think of any recent incident that might have influenced Charlotte's curiosity. I included this incident in my daily notes to Mr. Thomas. He looked extremely skeptical and couldn't believe that Charlotte could have typed that out to me. I wouldn't let his continuing pessimism deter me in the least. I knew she was communicating even if the classroom teacher didn't believe me. It hurt me to know that this teacher whom I had worked with for almost two years wouldn't accept that Soma had opened a window for Charlotte and that I had been able to continue and reach the "unreachable."

I continued with the questions…

"What can I do so we work together better?" BE THE TEACHER AND MAKE ME WORK

I would use this proclamation many times later when Charlotte was getting lazy. It would always produce a big smile from her and she'd get to work. "Be the teacher and make me work. You said it Charlotte. I'm just following your advice. Let's get going. Chop, Chop. Come on, I'm getting old!"

"How good is your memory?" I HAVE A GREAT MEMORY

"Is it better than most people have?" YES

Charlotte asked, "WHY DO PEOPLE CELEBRATE THEIR BIRTHDAYS" "Because they survived another year."

"How old are you?" 16

"How old am I?" 49 (Correct. How did she know that?)

"What can you do that nobody thinks you can do?" PERHAPS WALK FROM SCHOOL TO HOME

"What do I do that upsets you?" YOU GET IN MY FACE "What do you mean, I get in your face?" LIKE NOW "Is it because you are watching TV and I am bugging you?" YES I began walking away with a sad look on my face and looking very despondent. I started singing the song that Donkey sang from *Shrek*. "I'm all alone, nobody here besides me....." Charlotte cracked a big smile.

Later I continued with the questions.

"How do you know how to spell so well?" READING

"How does it feel to communicate for the first time in 16 years?" I FEEL FANTASTIC

"What day would you like the teenage girl to visit, Thursday or Friday?" EITHER DAY

The next day I continued.....

"How do you feel today?" SUPER

"What helped you the most in your breakthrough with communicating?" YOU She then grabbed the pencil from me and also wrote, "YOU" "Thank you Charlotte, that means a lot to me."

"How did I help you?" HUMOR

"What kind of teenager stuff would you like to learn about?" DATING

"What do kids do on dates?" KISSING

Charlotte was answering age appropriate questions. She was aware of so many things that had been thought of as beyond her grasp.

"What goal do you want to set for yourself this year?" TO TALK

"What expectations do I have for you this year?" TO HELP ME TALK

Charlotte typed this statement and I later discussed it with her folks. WHY DO TEENAGERS PRETEND TO WANT A RELATIONSHIP WITH A WOMAN OF THE NIGHT

"What is a woman of the night?" A PROSTITUTE

"What is a prostitute?" A WHORE   SELLS HER BODY   Like I said, she was aware of lots of things!

"What teenager wanted a relationship?" Charlotte typed out the name of one of her brothers.

"What makes you think he wants a relationship?" HE HAD A BOOK OF NUDE WOMEN

After discussing this with mom and dad, they remembered something that happened two years earlier. Charlotte had, indeed, caught her brother with a girly magazine and was very upset. She eventually took the magazine and burned it in the barbecue! It must have really upset her if the event still bothered her two years later.

"You've told me that folks with autism see only details." I then held my hand about five feet from her. "I see five fingers, what do you see?" I SEE FINGERPRINTS   Wow, no wonder she could see in the dark cave so well.

"What would you like to learn about today?" WHAT IS HER NAME

"The teenage girl who is coming to visit?" YES

"Clarissa."

Charlotte then asked, WHY DO PEOPLE TALK ABOUT ME

Dean A. Le Breton

"With respect to what?" AUTISM

"People are curious about autism and don't understand it very well. They see you flapping or grounding yourself and they talk about what they are seeing.

"Do you feel normal inside?" YES

"Has it been frustrating not to be able to communicate?" YES

"Is that the reason you have been so aggressive?" YES

Charlotte was supposed to meet Clarissa the following day. I reminded her and she smiled. The next morning was a different story. She seemed upset about something. During our Red Dot session, she broke the pencil and was grabbing at my hands and shirt. She wouldn't type anything when prompted. I threatened to call Clarissa and tell her not to come. Charlotte calmed immediately, which made me think that her behavior was due to the upcoming visit. "Are you scared to meet Clarissa?" YES EVERYONE IS MEAN   I assured her that Clarissa was a nice girl and wouldn't be mean. Clarissa was looking forward to meeting her. This assurance seemed to set her mind at ease and we continued our Red Dot work without any other problems.

Clarissa came in during lunch and Charlotte was a little apprehensive in the beginning. Clarissa gave her a teenage magazine, which Charlotte began to devour. She seemed to be using the magazine to avoid looking directly at her guest. Charlotte zipped through the magazine pretty fast. Then she started paying attention to Clarissa.

Clarissa asked Charlotte what she liked to do. WALK

"What do you like to do with your mom?" GO SHOPPING

Charlotte typed out WHY ARE PEOPLE MEAN

Clarissa said, "Some kids are mean, but most are nice. Sometimes they get in groups and can be mean."

WHAT DO YOU DO ON DATES

"I go with a group of kids, maybe five, and we have pizza, then go to a movie."

Clarissa gave Charlotte a CD full of teen music. THANK YOU

When Clarissa was leaving, Charlotte typed out   THANK YOU FOR COMING IN Then Charlotte said "Goodbye." That was so cool! She initiated spoken language to a peer. Charlotte really enjoyed meeting a peer and typed CAN SHE COME BACK   "Yes she can."

This was already an outstanding day, but it got even better. I told Charlotte that her story would make a good book. The way she had improved her behavior and started communicating was totally cool. "Can I write your story?" NO

"Do you want to write you own story?" YES

We began Charlotte's story that afternoon and would add to it when she felt like it. I could live with that. That first day she typed out five sentences for her first paragraph. It was February 23, 2006.

I HAVE AUTISM   AUTISTIC PEOPLE ARE VERY NICE THEY ARE HUMAN TOO   PEOPLE DON'T UNDERSTAND US   THEIR FEELINGS ARE VERY SIMILAR TO REGULAR PEOPLE

The next day she continued typing out her story on the alpha board.

DEAN IS TEACHING ME TO SAY LOTS OF THINGS   WE HAVE A GOOD RELATIONSHIP   WE CAME TOGETHER A FEW YEARS AGO   WE WORK TOGETHER AT SCHOOL WE STUDY VERY BEAUTIFULLY TOGETHER

I was surprised at how well she wrote. Not only were her words touching, she used the correct tense when referring to our meeting in the past. What else was locked up in her waiting to emerge?

Mr. Thomas continued to have doubts about the facilitated communication, thinking that Charlotte was taking queues from me when typing. He would ask, "Why can't she do it independently? Why doesn't she type it on the computer?" He would also state that the alpha board should be flat on a table rather than being held by me, and Charlotte should type without any prompting!

The doubting Mr. Thomas was frustrating for me because I knew that Charlotte had independent thoughts. She and I would converse with each other throughout the day. I would talk and she would type. If I were indeed "leading the witness" with queues, then that would mean I was talking to myself the whole day! That, of course, was not the case. Compounding the situation was the fact that Charlotte was very apprehensive about showing her communication skills to Mr. Thomas or to the three aides in the classroom. She would be typing away with me, then clam up when one of those people came near. I would plead with her, "Charlotte, will you show them you can type?" YES "Right now?" YES "If we go in there, you will type for them and show them your typing?" YES "Lets go." Feeling confident that she would finally type for them, I proclaimed that she was ready to show her talent. When the audience was assembled, Charlotte fumbled miserably. She wouldn't show them anything. Now I was frustrated not only with Mr. Thomas, but with Charlotte too.

I tried video taping Charlotte and I working together. A tripod was set up and I had a remote control to start the video camera. She looked up and saw the red light on the camera. She knew exactly what I was attempting to do and would have none of it.

Angie was very supportive of Charlotte's communication breakthrough. She contacted a professor friend who assured her that what Charlotte was doing was typical of facilitative communication. A bond would form with one person, and generalization with others would not take place. Angie was concerned that Mr. Thomas was putting Charlotte in a situation where she had to prove herself.

Phil visited our classroom to see how Charlotte was doing. He had seen my detailed documentation of the "Free Thinking Questions" which I sent home with Charlotte every day. Phil, Charlotte, and I went to the time out room and Charlotte did some Red Dot work. I asked Charlotte if she had any questions for her dad. She typed WHY WOULD YOU LOVE ME   Phil gave her a bunch of reasons in response, which made Charlotte happy. WHEN ARE WE GOING TO THE MOVIES "We can go this weekend. What do you want to see?" I WANT TO SEE ONE   Phil and I both were choked up a little, holding back tears. Charlotte was communicating with dad.

In an effort to verify that Charlotte's thoughts were hers and her typing was independent, Mr. Thomas had Angie write down questions about what Charlotte had done the previous night. I was to ask those questions of Charlotte, give the questions and answers to Mr. Thomas, and he would have Charlotte's responses verified by Angie or Phil. We hoped that this method of verification would be non-threatening to Charlotte.

The following Monday, Charlotte came in very frustrated. "Are you upset?" YES "Why are you frustrated?" BECAUSE I FEEL PISSED AT EVERYBODY "Why?" PEOPLE ARE MEAN

"What happened?" LAUGHED AT ME "Who laughed at you?" GIRLS "Where did it happen?" MOVIES At this point I felt she was disclosing an incident which happened over the weekend. The details I was getting from her would surely "prove" she could communicate. I continued, "What did dad do?" HE TALKED TO THEM "About what?" AUTISM "How many girls were there?" FIVE "How did you feel afterwards?" I WAS PISSED OFF THE WHOLE NIGHT

I was empathetic with her ordeal and let her know. I told her that the girls were immature and didn't understand autism. While I was sad that the event had happened, I was thrilled that Charlotte had shared verifiable data with me. I told Mr. Thomas the story's details knowing that Phil could validate their authenticity. When he talked to Phil, however, Mr. Thomas found out that they didn't even go to the movies over the weekend. None of Charlotte's story was true. I confronted Charlotte, "Did you tell Mr. Dean a joke?" She laughed and pointed to the big YES on the alpha board. "Real funny Charlotte." Charlotte was proving one thing to me. She could be a convincing manipulator. She knew about the attempt to verify her communication and she was not being very cooperative. She did things according to her own agenda, not ours. I could live with that. I also garnered more respect for her intellect. Weaving a story without any holes in it showed a high level of thinking process. I would be less gullible in the future.

Mr. Thomas often said that generalizing knowledge was very difficult for people with autism. They would just repeat facts but not know how to apply the knowledge. I felt that Charlotte could understand and utilize information. Since we had learned about the water cycle, I asked, "What do we do with water?" PUT WATER ON PLANTS DRINK WASH CLOTHES BOAT ON WATER Without a doubt, Charlotte was clearly demonstrating she knew what water could be used for. Another doubt bites the dust.

"Do you have any questions for me?" WHEN YOU WERE A TEENAGER SIMILAR TO ME DID PEOPLE TALK ABOUT AUTISTIC PEOPLE LIKE THEY WERE NOT THERE "I don't know. Kids with disabilities went to another school. I didn't know anyone with autism." This was an insightful question. She wanted to know about my past and attitudes towards autism. She was trying to compare the social attitudes over the years. This wasn't a question from a kid without any social awareness.

The Tates attended a meeting with Mr. Thomas and me one afternoon. I invited Charlotte to be there since we'd be talking about her. She came in and sat with the adults. We discussed what Charlotte was accomplishing at school and at home. Her behavior had been great in both environments. Mr. Thomas had no positive things to say about Soma's work or Charlotte's alpha board communication because it wasn't "research based or data driven." The following day, Phil wrote an E-mail to Mr. Thomas stating that the Tates felt there was an air of skepticism at the meeting. Phil said he was confident that Charlotte and I were communicating and we should focus on verifiable tasks to keep Charlotte honest. Don't take her typing as the gospel truth. I appreciated the show of support from Phil and Angie. In the long run, it was more important for mom and dad to know about Charlotte's abilities than Mr. Thomas.

Verifiable communication from Charlotte would prove to be hard to obtain. She had typed out stories with names of people, specific incidents, restaurant names, and dinner selections, which all turned out to be fictional. I had learned earlier not to get too excited about the information she provided. I would report Charlotte's stories to Mr. Thomas who then talked to or E-mailed the Tates. It might have been my imagination, but it seemed that he took pleasure in telling me that Charlotte's stories could not be verified.

My wife and I own three horses and board another two. After work, while feeding my horses and cleaning up the stalls, I generally relax, wind down, and contemplate what had transpired during the day. Ideas often popped into my head for future educational activities for Charlotte. I also used this time to reflect on Charlotte's amazing transformation from the "toughest kid to work with" to a person who was communicating, behaving, and showing a thirst for knowledge.

But I also thought about my frustration with her refusal to show other people her abilities. She was even hesitant to show her parents how well she could type. Whenever I told Mr. Thomas and colleagues about our conversations and successes, all I got were doubtful glances and looks of non-belief. Charlotte was not doing it "independently without prompting" and not generalizing communication with other people. I felt like an innocent prisoner who's claims fell on deaf ears. I knew she was communicating and I never wavered in being Charlotte's biggest advocate. I continued reporting what I personally witnessed coming out of Charlotte. It was all I could do.

CHAPTER 18

CHARLOTTE WAS AWARE AND INTERESTED in an aide's pregnancy. The aide, Susan, was six months along. I was hopeful that Charlotte would warm up to typing in front of Susan.

"How do you feel today?" I FEEL WONDERFUL

"Why don't you want to work with Susan?" I AM SCARED Susan assured her that she had nothing to be scared of.

"Why do you only want to work with me?" YOU TRY VERY HARD

"Do you have a question for Susan?" WHAT IS THE NATURE OF THE BABY

We weren't sure what she meant, but we told her it was a girl. The next day I asked her what she meant by "nature of the baby." HOW BIG IS IT I asked Susan, who said that they get an idea of size by using a sonogram camera to look inside the mommy. Charlotte typed MRI I asked, "MRI? What does that do?" TAKE A PICTURE "Where would you find an MRI machine?" HOSPITAL After Susan showed her a picture of a baby in the womb, Charlotte typed WHY IS THE BABY BREATHING THROUGH A CORD I explained about the baby being in a sac of water and getting air through the cord.

I thought that Susan would now be a believer. Charlotte typed in front of her using her own unique wording. I was wrong to assume. "She is not doing it independently. You are holding the alpha board

105

and it moves a little, giving her queues." I told her that when Charlotte hovers over a letter, I pronounce it. If the spelling makes no sense, I have her start again. "You can't prompt her so much." "I need to prompt her so she can stay focused." I knew that Mr. Thomas had been coaching my associates to look for things that would invalidate or cast doubts on Charlotte's communication skills. Susan was parroting his words and not believing her own eyes. I liked my colleagues and wanted to share my excitement over Charlotte's communication breakthrough. It was something to celebrate, but there was no party going on in our room. I was the only one there celebrating.

In an effort to get Charlotte to generalize with other people, Mr. Thomas came up with a plan to have my colleagues work with Charlotte on a daily basis. I was to leave the room and take Sam to PE. Each person would try to work with Charlotte for one hour each week. They were to use a series of YES/NO questions with obvious answers. For many weeks, Charlotte would choose all YES or all NO responses. Nobody was getting anything out of her. I would eagerly return from PE and read their summaries. Charlotte was fumbling. I believe that Charlotte was toying with them. They hadn't earned the right to communicate with her. After all, they put in a few minutes a week, while I had nurtured a strong working relationship with Charlotte throughout well over a thousand hours.

One day I told Charlotte an incredible story about a basketball player who had autism. He was substituted late in the game and scored 20 points in four minutes. Charlotte listened to me read the article and then we watched the video on a computer. She was very interested. I told her that people with autism could accomplish great things. Let him be an inspiration for you.

A few days later, Charlotte continued with "her" story.

WE LIKE TO HAVE A GOOD TIME IN SCHOOL   WE ARE JUST LOVING PEOPLE IN A MESSED UP BRAIN   WE ARE REAL PEOPLE WHO THINK JUST LIKE REGULAR PEOPLE   WE PERCEIVE THE WORLD DIFFERENTLY THAN REGULAR PEOPLE   WE SEE EVERYTHING THAT COMES INTO OUR VISION   WE SEE ONLY DETAILS   WE SEE VERY SMALL DETAILS

Her last entry in March was.....

WE ONLY WANT OUR SPACE ON EARTH   MANY MENTALLY RETARDED PEOPLE HAVE SOME ABILITY TO LEARN MORE THAN REGULAR PEOPLE KNOW   MANY AUTISTIC PEOPLE ONLY WANT TO BE TREATED LIKE REGULAR PEOPLE   THEY WANT TO BE WANTED AND LOVED

We continued with academic instruction using Soma's RPM method, and Charlotte was doing great both in learning and recalling this information. Teaching academics was important, but I concentrated more on communication. This would be a functional skill that would help her throughout her life. We did "Free Thinking Questions" daily. Over a few days in early March, we had these conversations.

"Why did you like to rip up video boxes?"   I DON'T KNOW "Why did you break my Pinocchio video?" (This episode had led to a big escalation outside the classroom. Mr. Thomas and I had to escort her back to the room.)   I WANTED TO THROW IT AWAY   "Why?" BECAUSE I WAS BORED WITH IT

"Why do you throw your coloring pages down the grid by the school wall?" BECAUSE I WANTED TO   I LIKED TO COLOR BUT IT WASN'T TEENAGER STUFF

"Why can't you type faster on the alpha board?" BECAUSE I WANT TO GET THE RIGHT SPELLING

We had ventured to the library and Charlotte typed out   HOW DOES THE LIBRARY HELPER KNOW THAT PEOPLE HAVE A BOOK CHECKED OUT   I explained about the bar code label and matching it up with a student's name.

"What can regular people learn from people who have autism?"   I WOULD TEACH THEM THAT AUTISTIC PEOPLE THINK LIKE THEM AND THAT WE ARE HUMAN TOO

Can you help me make a plan to help you to talk?   YES   "What prohibits you from talking? What goes on in your brain when you try to pronounce a word?" I TRY TO TALK BUT NOTHING HAPPENS THE WORDS CANT GO FROM MY BRAIN TO MY MOUTH

"Why don't you want to communicate with others using the alpha board?" BECAUSE THEY SCARE ME   "Why do they scare you?" THEY ARE MEAN   "Why have you chosen me to communicate with out of 6 billion people on earth?" BECAUSE YOU HAVE GIVEN ME HOPE "Hope for what?"   TO TALK "Why are you using the alpha board now and not before when we tried it?" BECAUSE I WANT TO FEEL SUPERIOR TOWARDS REGULAR PEOPLE

"Why have you been fooling everyone for so long?"   BECAUSE I COULD FOOL EVERYONE

I thought about that response for a long time.   She had fooled everyone for a long time. All the experts, doctors, psychologists, teachers, aides, etc. had been toyed with by Charlotte.

"Since you came back from Austin, Texas, you've been communicating very well. How did Soma help you?"   SHE WORKED ME HARD

"Were you afraid of her?" YES That is hilarious as Charlotte towers over the very petite Soma!

"You said you wanted to go to college yesterday. Tell me what you know about college." THERE ARE SMART KIDS THERE "You need to pass some tests to get into college. Not every regular person goes to college after high school. Could you pass those tests if you studied?" YES "You would have to prove to regular people how smart you really are. Could you do that?" YES

"Why are you afraid to show regular people how smart you are? You should be very proud of your abilities." THERE ARE NICE PEOPLE THAT I WILL TALK TO

"How close are you to being a regular person?" I AM REALLY CLOSE

Charlotte had told me about seeing the movie, "Eight Below". She gave me lots of details about the movie. She knew it took place in Antarctica with eight dogs. They ate whale meat, and a helicopter helped save them. She knew that a meteor had landed and that the weather was freezing. When asked, her parents said she hadn't seen the movie, but she did see "March of the Penguins." When I asked her about her tale, she said she was joking again. I asked how she knew the details of the movie, and she typed I SAW A PREVIEW.

More free thinking questions...

"What did you think of me when I used to dress up for you when you got off the bus?" REALLY STUPID "But you thought it was funny?" YES

"What can I do to help you calm down if you feel like escalating? Can I help you?" YES BE STRONG AND HELP ME RELAX "How?" BE OPEN MINDED AND USE YOUR GOOD SENSE

"What is the best way for you to learn something?" TALK TO ME "Can you absorb information by reading?" YES "What is better, hearing or reading?" HEARING

"What do you like?" I LIKE EVERYTHING ABOUT LEARNING

CHAPTER 19

MY MOTHER AND BROTHER FROM Alaska had come to visit me in the classroom. I introduced them to Miss Tate. Charlotte had a question for my mom. WHAT KIND OF PEOPLE LIVE IN ALASKA "Eskimos with dark skin and dark hair."

She asked my brother a question after I told her he was a hunter. WILL YOU BE WEARING A GUN "No."

"Do you have another question for my mother?" WHY IS DEAN SO WONDERFUL "Because he loves working with you and wants you to do well in school."

WHY ARE YOU IN IDAHO "For a visit to Dean's family," Mom replied.

Later that day Charlotte inquired...

WHY DID YOU BRING YOUR FAMILY TO SEE ME "They just flew into Boise and I wanted to say hi to them. I also wanted them to meet my student."

YOUR BROTHER IS SMALLER THAN YOU "Yes. Do you think he is older than me?" HE LOOKS OLDER THAN YOU "Yes he is."

I thought it was important that Charlotte meet my mother. That sent a message to Charlotte that she was not just my student, but an important person in my life. I thought it was great that Charlotte would even think of posing some of those questions. I also was proud of Charlotte for typing in front of strangers. This was great because it helped her to generalize communication efforts. Generalizing was a vitally important goal that I had for Charlotte.

In an effort to help Charlotte realize the importance of communicating with other people, I asked her this question:

"What would happen to you if I died? Would you be able to work and communicate with other nice people?" I WOULD FEEL VERY BAD YES

I was pleased that she felt she would be able to continue her communication efforts if I was out of the picture.

"What are some things that regular people do that you won't be able to do because of the autism?" REGULAR PEOPLE CAN LAUGH BETTER THAN ME "Are things that regular people laugh at funny?" YES

"What are some things that regular people do that you think are cool?" FEEL PEOPLES FEELINGS OF LOVE

The next day we continued our "Free Thinking Questions."

"How can you demonstrate more of your autistic memory talents?" I CAN REMEMBER STORIES READ TO ME

"What things have we done that have helped you talk?" WE TALK TO EACH OTHER A LOT

"What other things do you think will help you talk? Do flashcards help?" YES

"How accurate have I been when writing down your answers, questions, or statements from the alpha board?" VERY ACCURATE

"Why do you twirl around when walking?" I TWIRL TO RELAX

"How does grounding and flapping relax you?" IT PROBABLY RELAXES MY BRAIN

"Why did you throw away glue sticks before they were completely used up?" BECAUSE I WANT TO REMOVE IT FROM THE TUBE

Academically, Charlotte was doing very well. I would read her a seventh grade "Read Naturally" story and then ask her comprehension questions about the story. She would circle the multiple choice or write the answer for the fill-in questions. Topics included the planets of our solar system, the seven ancient wonders of the world, and architectural feats, such as The Eiffel Tower and The Golden Gate Bridge. Sometimes we'd sit together to read a story and at other times she would be standing and flapping while watching TV.

I didn't particularly like it when she was watching TV while I was reading, but she said she could do both at the same time. She proved it to me by getting the correct answers to my questions over and over. I was now convinced that she was an auditory learner as well as a visual learner.

An Educational Psychologist from Boise State University, Dr. Larry Rogien was doing some work at the junior high school. I had attended a presentation of his during a district in-service day. During his presentation, he mentioned self-esteem several times. During a break, I shared with Dr. Rogien some of Charlotte's accomplishments, including communication with the alpha board. I shared that her first question had something to do with self-esteem....WHY DO PEOPLE THINK I AM STUPID. We continued chatting and he congratulated me on helping to facilitate her communication breakthrough. At a later date, I happened to see Dr. Rogien in the hallway at the junior high, and he said that he would be interested in meeting Charlotte and seeing us work together. I said, "Great, but you'd better clear it with Mr. Thomas." He informed me that this would not be necessary because he had been given permission from the vice principal to visit all the programs at the junior high.

Dr. Rogien came to our classroom in the middle of March and I introduced him to Mr. Thomas. I had let Mr. Thomas know of the pending visit, but he seemed a little standoffish. Perhaps this was because Dr. Rogien hadn't contacted him personally. Dr. Rogien and I quickly left to visit with Charlotte. After introductions, I took out the alpha board and asked Charlotte if she had any questions. YES WAS DEAN IN YOUR CLASS   Dr. Rogien replied, "Yes." I then read a "Read Naturally" story about the ancient Roman Coliseum. Charlotte answered five questions in front of him. She missed the question about the capacity of the Coliseum. She had answered 50,000 instead of 60,000. When I asked her why she missed it she typed out MISTAKE. She did do a subtraction problem, 80AD minus 69AD, to figure out how long it took to build the Coliseum.

It was a nice visit and Charlotte seemed to enjoy herself. She did great. Since Charlotte had typed in front of so few people, I asked her why she had done it for Dr. Rogien. She typed out   HE WAS NICE AND LOOKED HAPPY   This "nice" and "happy" attitude was a continuing litmus test for Charlotte to use as an evaluation tool prior to communicating with people. Dr. Rogien wanted to return in a few weeks to observe us working together. I could tell that Mr. Thomas was not happy with the impromptu visit, so I re-emphasized to Dr. Rogien about contacting him prior to the next visit. I didn't want anything to stand in the way of trying to get Charlotte to broaden her communication skill and generalize with other people.

More "Free Thinking Questions" from the middle of March:

"Why don't you want to type on the computer?" BECAUSE I WANT TO TALK TO YOU

"Can you go faster when pointing (typing) on the alpha board?" I CAN GO A LITTLE FASTER

"Do you remember when Mr. Thomas and I were at your house when you got off the bus?" YES

"What were your thoughts when you saw us?" I'M IN TROUBLE WITH SCHOOL

"Were you surprised to see us?" YES

Charlotte had a statement. I WANT TO READ ON WOMEN THAT HAVE AUTISM

"Will you do that with your mother?" YES

There was one day where Charlotte showed all three of the other aides her typing ability. She started out by typing WHY ARE YOU BLACK to an aide. He responded, "Because I am." I chimed in, "His parents were black." Charlotte turned to him and typed out WERE THEY BLACK "Yes." She continued WERE THEY NICE "Yes." It seemed important to Charlotte that people needed to be nice. Charlotte asked four questions to another aide about her house and family. She then asked Susan about her baby. WHO WILL WATCH THE LITTLE BABY WHEN YOU ARE HERE Susan responded that she would be quitting work and staying with the baby. Susan still thought that I was directing Charlotte's responses. Charlotte would hover over a letter for a few seconds and I would prompt her to touch it if it was the right letter and the one she wanted. "She's not doing it independently." I countered with, "So it is just a coincidence that she hovers over letters that spell out words and sentences that make perfect sense for the conversation taking place?" She reverted to the old standby that Mr. Thomas had used to discount Charlotte's communication breakthrough. "You're holding the alpha board and it should be flat on the table. You prompt her too much." I thought to myself that if she thought I was influencing or communicating for Charlotte, then why did she answer Charlotte's questions about her baby?

More free thinking questions......

"What questions should I be asking you that I haven't asked yet?" WHY DO AUTISTIC PEOPLE FEEL DIFFERENT

"Why do autistic people feel different?" WE DONT FEEL ANY DIFFERENT THAN REGULAR PEOPLE

"How can communicating with regular people help you in you life?" IT COULD HELP ME WITH EVERYTHING   I COULD TELL THE DOCTOR WHAT HURTS   MAKE FRIENDS   I WANT A BOYFRIEND

"If you want to start a conversation with a regular person, what do you need to do?"

GET THE ABC BOARD TYPE THE MESSAGE   WAIT FOR THE REPLY

"That's totally correct. You need to do it with other people too, not just me!"

Well, she certainly knew what to do. Maybe she didn't have the confidence to do it. She had said many times that she was scared to type with other people.

She continued with "Charlotte's Story."

WE NEED TRAINING   I COULD HELP TO TEACH STUDENTS HOW TO UNDERSTAND THE WAYS OF

REGULAR PEOPLE   MAYBE THE AUTISTIC STUDENTS COULD GO TO YOUR HOUSE AND RIDE HORSES

My wife and I have talked about doing this. We have a "bombproof" horse that is about 30 years old and would be great for teaching kids about horses. My wife is an English language tutor, and with my special education experience, we thought we could entertain disabled children with the horses. We could also have an afternoon program where the kids could learn Spanish. Maybe someday......

She continued.....

I AM TALKING A LOT   I AM USING AN ALPHA BOARD TO COMMUNICATE IT MAKES ME WANT TO ASK QUESTIONS FOR PEOPLE TO ANSWER   I FEEL TREMENDOUS WHEN I COMMUNICATE WITH OTHER PEOPLE LOTS OF PEOPLE THINK AUTISM MEANS THAT PEOPLE WHO HAVE IT CANT DO ANYTHING   ONLY A FEW PEOPLE WITH AUTISM MAY HAVE SEVERE AUTISM WITH OTHER DISABILITIES VERY FEW PEOPLE WITH AUTISM UNDERSTAND THEIR EFFORTS TO READ WORDS MANY PEOPLE THINK THAT PEOPLE WITH AUTISM USUALLY UNDERSTAND THAT THEY DON'T KNOW MUCH ABOUT ANYTHING THIS IS NOT TRUE AUTISTIC PEOPLE KNOW THAT THEY THINK UNUSUALLY

This was the last entry that Charlotte made for "her" story. I find it very insightful. Her higher self-esteem is evident when she talks about communicating with other people. She is also saying that people with autism are wrongly perceived as not understanding anything. It appears that they are aware of many, many things. They are also aware of their disability and that they think differently. When I witnessed Charlotte typing out this story in her own words, I felt very privileged to be in her company. It still amazes me that this "unreachable, unteachable" young lady could have and share such intelligent and insightful thoughts. I shared my enthusiasm with my family during dinner conversation. Their grasp of autism and what Charlotte was accomplishing was somewhat limited. I'd describe some of the things Charlotte had been doing and typing out. "Wow dad, that's cool. Pass the carrots please." At least I got a little acknowledgement from someone other than the Tates. They knew what was going on and were very happy and thankful for my efforts. Mr. Thomas' position on Soma's RPM method and Charlotte's communication breakthrough, however was still unchanged.

In the classroom, Charlotte typed for two more folks. Gary Washington, her former behavior interventionist, came in and was excited to see Charlotte. It had been one and a half years since she had bitten him. When I told him she was now communicating, he looked somewhat amazed. We left the side of the portable where the adults had hung out and ventured to the side where the kids were. I brought the alpha board with me too. Charlotte looked happy to see Gary and turned off the TV when prompted. Gary was impressed that she did that without protesting. Gary said hello and made some small talk. I asked him if he had any questions for Charlotte. "What is the color of your shirt?" Charlotte quickly typed out PINK. Big old Gary just stared with a vacant look. He couldn't believe it. We talked later. "Wow, that's incredible. She looks so calm and happy." I replied that since she had been communicating, she had become happier and more compliant. A new image of Charlotte was replacing some of the past ones in Gary's head.

Charlotte also typed for the speech teacher. The three of us sat together on the couch and I quizzed Charlotte on previous lessons.

"Who is buried in the pyramids?"   KING

"What country are they in?"   EGYPT

"Where was Columbus from?"   ITALY

"What are the names of his ships?"   NINA   PINTA   SANTA MARIA

We also did a lot of accurate YES/NO questions. The speech teacher was impressed and excited about this communication breakthrough. As I mentioned earlier, Charlotte had worked with her before and liked her. Liking a person seemed to be a common thread when it came to Charlotte showing her communication abilities. I asked the speech teacher to tell Mr. Thomas what she had observed. She said she would, but I didn't hear a thing from him that day.

We continued the Red Dot work over the next few days and discussed Machu Picchu, the human digestive system, the nervous system, the five senses, Australia, Europe, Easter Island, North America, South America, birds, and more on Egypt. The day after each lesson, we would review the material. She had excellent recall and rarely missed a question. She continued to pronounce lots of words from flashcards too.

Another breakthrough Charlotte had was with the analog clock. She had done well with full and half hours, but quarter and three quarter hours had been hard for her to identify. I had a clock and would set the arms at various positions. She could choose from a list of times on a piece of paper. If the answer wasn't there, Charlotte would type it out on the number side of the alpha board. She would nail all of the questions every time.

I talked about how each number on the clock represented five minutes and I then quizzed her. "If the minute hand is on five, how many minutes after the hour would that be?" 25 she typed. "Great Charlotte. That is correct! How about if the minute hand is on the eight?" She typed out 40. "Nice job. Correct again." We also discussed one-minute increments, which she seemed to grasp. I stated, "There are 60 minutes in one hour. How many minutes are in two hours?" 120 she typed. "Five hours?" 300 was her reply. "Ten hours?" 600 was typed. "Super job Tate."

Later that same day I was reminded that Charlotte's misbehaviors were just below the surface. We were working on pronouncing sounds that various letters and combinations of letters make. Out of the blue, she bopped me twice on the top of my head. I told her to stop, but she continued to grab at my shirt. I told her that her actions were unacceptable and gathered up my things and left the room. She began to moan loudly. I returned a few minutes later and discussed the topic of frustration with her. I told her that regular people used their words instead of their fists. "Do you understand?" YES We finished the lesson without any other incidents.

Prior to the spring break, Charlotte demonstrated an affinity for working with numbers. In my mind, this bordered on Savant-like abilities. We were working with groups of five. I asked her to count her fingers and toes. She typed out 20. "Count yours and mine together." 40 "If you had five people?" 100 "That is really good Charlotte!" She beamed with pride. "How about five people just counting toes?" 50 "What if you had nine sets of five?" 45 She had never done much with adding and subtracting for me so I was amazed that she could multiply so easily. At that point I queried, "Are you good with numbers?" YES "Did Soma teach you?" NO "You knew numbers before we went to Austin?" YES I continued with multiplying...."What is 112 times 3?" 336 was her reply. "423 times 5?" 2115. "Wow, Charlotte. You are pretty good!" I was pretty sure that was the answer when I did it in my head, but to be sure, I did it on a calculator. Sure enough, I was staring at a display that read 2115.

When another aide ventured in to our side of the portable, I stated what Charlotte had done. "Let me see that calculator." He pushed a few buttons and said, "What is 463 times 5?" Charlotte typed out a 2, then hesitated. "Come on Charlotte, finish it!" I said. Nothing doing. Charlotte would not continue in front of the aide. Once again, Charlotte was promoting the assertion that Mr. Dean was losing it.

CHAPTER 20

IT WAS A NICE SPRING break for me. That's a time for me to get the ranch ready for spring and summer. I worked on the gardens and the irrigation system that waters the pastures. While I was doing these chores, I thought about what had been happening at school. Charlotte was communicating mainly with me. She had typed in front of "nice" people including Clarissa, the speech teacher, my mother and brother, her father and mother, Dr. Rogien from BSU, Gary Washington, and the three aides who were in denial. All of those folks except for the aides accepted that Charlotte was, indeed, showing the ability to communicate. None of them commented that I was facilitating too much or influencing what Charlotte was typing. I had a few people in my corner. I couldn't wait to return to school to continue this amazing breakthrough with my student. I was confident in her communication skills and in my ability to continue to get her to express herself.

There was excitement in the air when Charlotte returned from spring break. She was happy and seemed ready to continue coming out of her 16-year-old "shell." She would definitely come out in the next few days.

"How was your spring break?" IT WAS GREAT

We started out with some free thinking questions…..

"Why do we have calendars?" SO WE CAN FIGURE OUT WHAT DATE THINGS HAPPEN

"Why do we have clocks?" SO WE CAN KNOW WHAT TIME IT IS

"What did you like about the book you read with your mom about Jessica Park?" SHE HAD AUTISM   SHE DIDNT TALK SHE OVERCAME AUTISM   SHE OVERCAME AUTISM BY WORKING HARD

"How old is she?" IN HER 40s

"Where does she work?" MAILROOM AT COLLEGE

"What does she paint?" (I had heard of her artistic abilities) BUILDINGS   I looked up Jessica Park on the Internet and checked on Charlotte's responses. The answers were correct.

In an effort to get Charlotte to generalize with other people, I jumped on the bus with her one afternoon. "Do you have anything to say to Scott (the driver)?"   CAN HE TAKE A DETOUR TO MY HOUSE   "Scott, do you know what she is talking about?" Scott and the bus monitor were laughing. He explained that the previous day he missed the turnoff to Charlotte's house and had to drive up the road quite a way to turn around. He had proclaimed, "Charlotte, we are taking a detour." I relayed this story to Mr. Thomas. I had no prior knowledge of that event, but the bus driver did. Charlotte had independently thought and typed out an event from the previous day, and the bus driver verified it. I anxiously awaited Mr. Thomas' reply. I might as well have waited until Christmas because there was no response or anything that implied that he believed Charlotte could, in fact, be communicating. Something special was happening in his classroom, yet he would not be part of it. It was like he had blinders on and couldn't see the miraculous transformation that was happening right beneath his nose. I couldn't understand why a teacher wouldn't be more supportive.

Charlotte continued to impress me with her talent for numbers. She did the following in her head, and I verified the answers with a calculator.

"What is 428 times 5?" 2140 "183 times 3?" 549 "315 times 7?" 2205
"163 times 4?" 652   Finally I tried to stump her with a really hard
calculation. "What is 4,261 times 4?" I barely had time to sit back in
the chair when she banged out 17,044. I checked her answer and it was
correct. "Charlotte Tate, you are amazing!"

Her math talents had inspired me to begin a conversation about
special talents that some people with autism possess. "Some people with
autism can count many items quickly. Can you do this?" YES   I was
eating my lunch and showed her the contents of my Tupperware. It
contained leftover rice and green peas. "How many peas are there?" She
glanced at the container and quickly typed out 14. I counted them up
and sure enough, there were 14 peas. "That was pretty good Charlotte.
Do you want more problems?" YES   I went to the other room and
retrieved some golf tees of various colors. "You ready?" YES   I tossed
them on the ground and Charlotte took a quick look. She typed out
54 on the number side of the alpha board. "54 tees. Is that correct?"
NO "How many?" She typed out 53. I counted them up in groups of
10. There were five groups of 10 with three left over for a total of 53!
"Charlotte, you are doing great." I took a handful away and tossed the
rest down on the rug. "How many now?" She typed out 33. I counted
them and only got 30. "Charlotte, there was only 30. What happened?"
MISTAKE

I was feeling pretty good about what my student was demonstrating
and asked her if she liked this "game." YES "Do you want more?" She
clearly said, "More!" I ventured into the other portable to find the bucket
with various shapes, sizes, and colors of buttons. I returned and dumped
them on the ground an queried, "How many buttons?" She typed out
80. As I counted them, I soon realized there were far fewer than 80
buttons. "Charlotte, would you like to guess again?" This time she typed
out 53. I arrived at 54 for my tally. Pretty close I thought. I finally got

some puffballs and tossed them to the ground. "How many balls?" 27
She was correct. There were 27 red, blue, yellow, and white puffballs.
Wow!

"Charlotte, you are showing me some pretty neat things. Do you
have other autistic talents?" YES   I CAN READ PRETTY FAST
AND KNOW WHAT I READ

"Would you like to show me your talent?" YES

I retrieved a World History book and went to a page on Egypt. "How
many seconds do you need to read the page?" She typed out 3. "I'll give
you five seconds." After five seconds, I took the book and began quizzing
her. "What is a vizier?" STEWARD OF THE WHOLE LAND
That's what the book said! I continued, "What is mummification?"
A PROCESS OF SLOWLY DRYING A DEAD BODY TO
PRESERVE IT FROM ROTTING   Correct again! "What did
workers remove?" LIVER LUNGS STOMACH INTESTINES
Same order as the book! "They placed them in special.......?" JARS
she banged out. "They covered the corpse with a ....?" NATURAL
SALT   "Wow Charlotte, that was outstanding. You are amazing!" She
was feeling very good about herself at this point and I wanted to keep
the ball rolling.

I mentioned previously that the second half of her ninth grade was
almost unbelievable. Her savant-like abilities were very special, but not
uncommon for people with autism. Some examples of savant abilities
would be musical talent, phenomenal memorization, (phone books or
maps), painting or drawing well, having strong numeric abilities, or
being able to count items quickly. Charlotte's math, counting, and fast
memorization skills all fall into this amazing category.

CHAPTER 21

IN ORDER TO PREPARE YOURSELF for the next dissertation of Charlotte's abilities, I strongly suggest that you put on a seatbelt and enjoy the ride. I am not a Stephen King type author. He can delve into his imagination and write the stuff he is known to be so good at. I have only written about things that I've observed first hand or read about from documentation. The next narrative stays true to such "first hand account" information.

I asked Charlotte again, "What other autistic talents do you have?" I CAN LOOK AT PEOPLE AND KNOW WHAT THEY ARE THINKING

OK, I always thought Charlotte could read people's expressions or emotions from their faces and body language.

"Are you telling me that you can read minds?" YES "Really?" YES

"Will you show me your talent?" YES

"I'm thinking of a color." I wrote "blue" on a piece of paper out of her view. She typed BLUE.

Maybe she got lucky. "I'm thinking of another color." I wrote down "brown". BROWN Now she has my undivided attention. "I'm thinking of something." I wrote down "water" making absolutely sure she couldn't see my writing and I thought of the word "water." She quickly typed out WATER At this point, I'm thinking that something incredible is happening and I am part of it. Charlotte is sharing her

127

biggest secret with me, not anyone else. I'm feeling pretty honored and privileged. Three correct answers in a row were unbelievable enough, but could she do even more? Oh yeah.

We did four more together and she nailed each one without hesitation. TURTLE FOUR COMPUTER LIGHT Correct on all accounts! Could she do two word thoughts? I looked around the room, noticed a "Toy Story" poster, and I thought of the character on the poster. WOODY POSTER Those were the exact words I had thought of. She had just reeled off eight out of eight thoughts that were in my head. I did two more with her. I thought of "house" and "cat". HOUSE CAT

After I caught my breath, I realized that it was my duty and responsibility to report my newly discovered observations of her talents to Mr. Thomas. Was I looking forward to it? Certainly not. He still didn't acknowledge the fact that she was communicating her own thoughts by pointing to letters on an alpha board. Not much chance of him believing this.

I excitedly reported what I had witnessed to Mr. Thomas. I told him about the savant-like demonstrations and the mind reading. He predictably looked at me with disbelief. The other aides were in the room too and their looks went along with Mr. Thomas' assessment. Well, I had fulfilled my obligation, but there were no believers in that room.

I returned to Charlotte and asked her if I could tell her parents what she could do. YES

She then typed out, YOU LOOK PRETTY AMAZED "Actually, Charlotte, I am way passed amazed. What you did is unbelievable. Regular people can't do what you just did. You are an amazing human being and I love working with you! Thank you for sharing your autistic talents with me." She had a big smile on her face.

The savant-like demonstrations and all the mind reading happened toward the end of a Tuesday. I was floating on cloud nine when Charlotte departed on the bus. It occurred to me that Charlotte's stemming was non-existent while she was doing the savant and mind reading activities. She was focusing on demonstrating her talents for me and I guess she didn't have time or a need to stem. I couldn't wait for the next day.

Wednesday was another day of astounding displays of her mind reading capabilities. She typed out what I was thinking time after time and was always accurate. I brought a pack Zenner cards, which are used for validation of extra sensory perception (ESP). The cards have the symbols of a star, three wavy lines, a square, a circle, or an addition "plus" sign. The "sender" looks at a card and the "receiver" attempts to identify what was sent. For Charlotte, I placed the five different cards face up, in front of her. I shuffled the deck and explained the "game" we were going to play. I was going to look at a card and think the symbol on it. Charlotte would then point to one of her five cards. She missed the first card, but then reeled off four correct answers of what symbol I had "sent".

I asked her if she could answer a question that I asked with my thoughts. YES I thought in my head, "What color are my eyes?" She typed out GREEN. Correct. I thought, "What is my street address?" She typed out 2636. "Charlotte, you are incredible!"

I asked her if she would show Mr. Thomas and the others her wonderful autistic talent. I was surprised when she typed out YES. She seemed caught up in the whole thing, and I thought she was ready to finally show the non-believers. We went to the other side of the portable and I was confident that she was going to blow them away. Once again, Charlotte fumbled in front of an audience. Mr. Thomas was now sizing me up for a white straight jacket. Oh well, I believed.

I had written some new "Free Thinking Questions" based on her newly revealed talent.

"Can you read my thoughts from my house to yours?" NO

"How far can you read my thoughts?" PRETTY FAR AWAY

"How far?" FROM THIS ROOM TO THE SCHOOL

"You can read my thoughts from that far away?" YES

"When you are reading thoughts, do you sense one or two words, or the whole sentence in a thought?" THE WHOLE THOUGHT

"What happens when there are two or three people thinking?" I CAN TAKE THEM APART

"Can you block out thoughts?" NO

"Does grounding block out or protect you from thoughts?" NO

"Can you read Andy or Sam's thoughts?" YES

"How about other people with autism?" YES I CAN PICK UP ON MOST PEOPLE

"Can you read animals' thoughts?" NO

"How do you perceive thoughts?" REALLY EASY

"Do you have any other autistic abilities or talents?" NO

"Why did you say you would show Mr. Thomas and the others your superior talent, and then you clam up?" I UNDERSTAND THEY WANT TO BELIEVE BUT THEY HAVE DOUBTS ABOUT STUPID PEOPLE

"What stupid people?" PEOPLE WITH AUTISM

"What thoughts from regular people confuse you or upset you?" WHEN THEY ARE MEAN AND STUPID TOWARDS AUTISTIC PEOPLE

"What activities can we do together that you think would challenge your brain?" UNDERSTANDING A THOUGHT AND TALKING ABOUT IT

"A thought from whom?" AN AUTISTIC PERSON

"What fun activities would you like to do?"   WE COULD TAKE A WALK

"How am I doing as your teacher?"   GREAT AND I AM HAPPY

Wow, Charlotte had shared lots of interesting information with me. It was a lot to digest, so I'm glad I wrote everything down as it was being revealed to me.

At lunchtime, it was pretty quiet with only an aide in one portable, and Charlotte and I in the other. Out of the three aides, this one was most open to the possibility that Charlotte was communicating, but he was still operating under the "Thomas" definition of independent communication. I went over to him and asked him to write down a word and think about it. He wrote it on a white board as I was returning to Charlotte. I yelled, "Are you thinking of the word?" "Yes," he replied. "OK Charlotte, what word is he thinking?" She didn't hesitate and typed out...HIS SCHOOL NUMBER   I queried, "His badge number?" YES   I yelled over to him, "Are you thinking of your badge number?" "No." "Charlotte, focus. What is he thinking?" This time Charlotte typed out the word ... SCHOOL. "Did you write down school?" This time he replied, "Yes, that's it!" I was praising Charlotte for showing someone else her talent when he came over to us. He looked a little surprised. I asked, "Well, what do you think?" "I think it was a lucky guess. Let's try another one." He wrote another word on the white board and I asked Charlotte to do her thing. Charlotte didn't type out anything, even though I was prompting her. Maybe she thought that luck had nothing to do with her answer and that the aide wasn't worthy of witnessing her talent. When there was doubt, Charlotte was out.

I wanted to test the range of Charlotte's ability and wondered if she could read thoughts in another language. I thought of the word escargot.

"Charlotte, what am I thinking." ESCARGOT   "Now what am I thinking?" I though of snail. She typed out......SNAIL.

I pondered what she had done and felt that she read thoughts like they were written on a blackboard. I'm pretty sure she didn't know what escargot meant, but she could read it off my mental "blackboard" just fine.

Charlotte was having fun showing me her abilities. Her whole demeanor was very positive. She was proud to finally have a stage to showcase her amazing ability. We did a few more things that day. I looked at her and thought, "Charlotte has big muscles." "What was I thinking?" BIG MUSCLES   I drew a fish in an aquarium and looked at the picture. "What did I draw?"   FISH IN SQUARE   I thought it interesting that she described the aquarium as a square, but that is what it looks like. I then drew a lady bug and when asked, she typed out LADY BUG

Sherri, the consulting teacher and one of the "original five" from room 17, came in for a quick visit. I didn't know if this visit had anything to do with me telling Mr. Thomas about Charlotte's amazing talents. I wasn't about to let the cat out of the bag and didn't offer to tell her anything about the last few days' happenings. I did show her Charlotte's typing ability. Sherri asked, "How do you feel today?" Charlotte typed out....I FEEL FINE   I left to go to PE with Sam while Sherri tried to use the alpha board with Charlotte, but had no success.

When I returned to the portables, I checked on the data that had been taken when Mr. Thomas and the aides had worked with Charlotte. They still had no success. This didn't surprise me as I felt that Charlotte was still toying with the unbelievers. This manipulating and lack of revealing herself to them reinforced my thinking that she had an above average intellect.

I grabbed the alpha board and headed off to quiz Charlotte about my thoughts during PE class. "During my walk, I thought of something. What was it?" PURPLE DONUT "In the gym, I looked at the record board. What did I send you?" ARM HANG RAYMOND SMITH "What did I think when a girl came into class late?" BRACES ON TEETH Amazing! All of her answers were 100% accurate. I followed up with two more questions. "Did you pick up on those thoughts as they were happening?" YES "Did you pick my brain just now as I asked you the questions and thought of the answers?" I DO IT BOTH WAYS

I needed some solid validation for what I was experiencing. Maybe I was going nuts and somehow I was tricking myself. Since Charlotte wouldn't show the non-believers in the classroom, maybe she would show another adult whom she liked and who had been nice to her. I came up with the idea of Walter, the in-house detention supervisor. Charlotte had known him for two and a half years. "Charlotte, will you show Walter your amazing talents?" YES

Charlotte and I walked over to the main building and found Walter's office. He was always pleasant to Charlotte and greeted her with a big, "Hi Charlotte!" I told him that Charlotte had been doing some amazing things for me but not for the others in the classroom. She said she'd do them for you. "Would you like to see her talents?" He enthusiastically replied, "Yes!"

I wrote down the word "ocean" on a sticky note and gave it to Walter. Charlotte was sitting on the ground in front of Walter's desk and was facing away from him. "What did I write down?" She typed out OCE then stopped. With a little prompting, she finished with AN. I then wrote a four digit number for Walter to look at. "What number did I write down?" She quickly and accurately typed out the four-digit number that I had written down. We now had Walter's attention.

"Charlotte, can we show him your reading memorization talent?" YES   I got a dictionary and had Charlotte look at one column for five seconds. I gave the book to Walter and asked him to choose a word in the column. She typed out the definition for that word exactly as it was written in the dictionary. She did the same thing for a second selected word. On a third word, she did not have the same success as with the previous words.

I then retrieved a classroom book and had Charlotte scan a page. Walter selected a sentence and read the first few words. Charlotte then typed out the rest of the sentence verbatim. Walter selected another sentence, and Charlotte nailed the ending again.

I asked Walter to write down a word and concentrate on it. "Charlotte, what did he write?"   GOD   Walter had written down the word Easter. Walter is a religious man and said that Easter and God are definitely related in his mind. Pretty close. Walter then wrote down a body part. Charlotte typed out   LEG   Walter said he was thinking of heart. "What happened Charlotte?" MISTAKE   Finally, I asked Walter to write down a number. Charlotte and I were both unable to see what he was writing. Charlotte typed out "6." Then she hovered over "7," but finally went back to "6." "She went to six really fast, then moved to seven before finally settling on six. What number did you write down?"   "I wrote down six, but six and seven are my favorite numbers!" He thanked us for showing him Charlotte's talents. He was impressed. Charlotte and I returned to the room feeling proud of ourselves. I praised her all the way back. She had done great and I was relieved to know that I wasn't going nuts.

When we returned to the classroom, Charlotte relaxed with some TV. I relaxed by writing up the events that had transpired in Walter's office. I had brought back the sticky notes, pieces of paper, and the notebook that had descriptions of what Charlotte had done. She had done a lot of things for Walter so well that I asked her if she would show Mr. Thomas. (Will I never learn?) She typed out...YES.

I reported everything to Mr. Thomas that had happened with Walter. With this new revelation of verification, I expected a little more than what I received. Mr. Thomas, stoic and skeptical as ever, managed an "Uh huh." I had him now, I thought. Charlotte was finally ready to show him and the aides. I went to Charlotte to verify her intent. "Are you really ready to show them your talents?" YES "Right now, we are going to walk in there and show them your talents?" YES Finally, I felt confident that she was indeed ready to show the unbelievers.

With me, she had been nailing one-word thoughts, so I asked Mr. Thomas to write one word. He humored me and wrote a word on a white board. "Think the word," I instructed. "Charlotte, what is the word?" Nothing. "Come on Charlotte, you said you would show him." She fumbled around pointing at various letters that meant nothing. "She just showed Walter a bunch of stuff." Charlotte continued to fumble and finally clamed up. Charlotte really didn't want to show Mr. Thomas or the aides her communication or mind reading ability. They just didn't believe that people with autism had any talents and that seemed to be Charlotte's criteria for allowing folks to witness her amazing feats. "I don't know what is wrong." Mr. Thomas then boomed out, "She's not doing it because she can't do it!" Storm clouds had been brewing between us ever since I had been claiming that Charlotte was capable of communicating her thoughts. Now lightening was about to strike.

Mr. Thomas stated that the situation with Charlotte had become disruptive to his classroom and that I would be receiving a letter telling me to stop all activities associated with mind reading or testing her so-called savant abilities. I wasn't shocked by his proclamation, but I still couldn't believe that a teacher would be averse to celebrating or at least, investigating thoroughly, the claims made by a trusted associate who had no past history of mental illness. Charlotte was a treasure chest full of insights into the mind of a person with autism. What a waste of opportunity not to pursue what she had to offer the world. She was coming out of a self-imposed 16-year exile, and Mr. Thomas was slamming her cell door shut.

I stayed as calm as possible and reiterated that she was, indeed, communicating and could, in fact, read minds. I asked him to talk to Walter who had witnessed her abilities. Mr. Thomas remarked loudly, "I don't have to talk to him!" This was happening in front of the other three aides and they were looking uncomfortable. I continued, "What are you afraid of? Please talk to Walter." "No, you are going to get the letter!" Then I did something that I had never done in my life. I begged. "I beg you, talk to Walter. He can verify the things I am claiming." After three or four minutes of going back and forth, he agreed to talk to Walter.

I anxiously awaited his return, knowing that Walter would be able to convince him of Charlotte's abilities. When he returned, he said that Walter validated some of the things I had said. Walter said that Charlotte was accurate about half of the time. I thought she had done much better than that, but didn't chime in with my assessment. In any case, I expected a retraction of the letter and support for trying to find out more about Charlotte's abilities. Once again, my expectations would not come to fruition. "You are still getting the letter!"

I got the letter prior to going home that day. He wanted me to read it at home and discuss it with him the next morning.

Basically, the letter indicated that Mr. Thomas didn't believe that Soma's process had opened any doors for Charlotte with respect to a communication breakthrough. According to school policy, we were to stick to the Individualized Education Plan (IEP), and use only data-driven and research-based processes and materials. Mr. Thomas' interpretation of this policy was that the Soma method, mind reading, and savant testing had no place or validity in our classroom. In addition, trying to have Charlotte "perform" for other people was a violation of her privacy. I was unaware that utilizing an alpha board and trying to generalize communication with other people was "performing!" It was communicating. He stated that he was concerned with what Charlotte's parents would think. I deduced from that comment that he hadn't shared any of my recent claims through his daily communication notebook or by e-mail with the Tates.

The following morning, I met with Mr. Thomas and told him that I would abide by his rules. I added, however, that Charlotte was communicating and had the other amazing abilities, which I had referred to, but that the school district was evidently unprepared to handle a student of her caliber. He told me that I was to work only on her IEP goals.

CHAPTER 22

I WENT HOME THAT AFTERNOON and pondered the situation. What do I do when I know that something amazing is happening, but the person who needs to be convinced of it does not believe me? After considering my options, I decided to contact Charlotte's parents. I thought I had a moral obligation to let them know how special their daughter was, even if I had to bypass the classroom teacher. What if I died suddenly? They would never know the truth about what Charlotte was capable of. As a behavior interventionist, I was supposed to keep a positive relationship with my student's parents. I had to be her advocate.

I talked to Angie that night and filled her in on recent events involving her amazing daughter. I cited many examples and waited for her response. "I always thought she might have that ability." It was such a relief to have her say that and not that she thought I was nuts. We continued talking for a while. Finally, I asked if I could come over to their house on Saturday to work with Charlotte in front of her and Phil. "Of course!" I had previously asked Charlotte if she would show her parents her amazing autistic talents and she had said YES. I had always let Charlotte be part of the decision-making process. I think it helped her to realize that I respected her and I knew that what she wanted mattered. She would be "performing" because she wanted to, not because Mr. Dean said to do it. I was thoroughly looking forward to the Saturday visit.

My son had a football game on Saturday morning and I planned on visiting the Tates after the game. I brought an egg carton which contained some farm fresh eggs, a small red dinosaur, and a blue ball. The lid of the carton was taped shut. In order to remove any suspicion that I had previously coached Charlotte, I also brought a piece of paper that had statistics from the game that my son had just played.

When I arrived, Phil and Charlotte were out doing some errands so Angie and I chatted. They returned in a few minutes and I asked Charlotte if she still wanted to show her parents her talents. YES was touched on the alpha board. I went to the refrigerator and retrieved the egg carton that I had brought.

"Charlotte, how many eggs are in the carton?" I thought of the answer. I turned the alpha board to the numbers side and Charlotte went right to the "4." "How many brown eggs?" Again I thought of the answer. She went to the "2." "How many white eggs?" She again touched "2." "What else is in the carton?" RED DINO   BLUE BALL   I opened the carton in front of the Tates and they looked at two brown eggs, two white eggs, a red dinosaur, and a small blue ball.

Angie hugged Charlotte for over a minute. Phil and I also hugged (but not for a minute.) It was a Kodak moment and very touching. They were both so proud of their daughter.

I then handed Phil the paper with my son's football statistics from that morning. I asked Charlotte these questions while I thought of the answers:

"How many touchdowns did he make?" Her finger pointed to "2."

"How many interceptions did he make?" Her finger hovered over "2" again.

"How many catches did he make?" The finger went to the "3."

"What was the final score of the game?" 32-18

"What is the name of his team?" RED RAIDERS

I glanced up at Phil who was holding the paper in his hand. He just stood there looking pretty amazed at what had just happened. "You're amazing Charlotte!" he quipped.

We all took a breather and then discussed what had transpired. When you are exposed to something that is supposed to be impossible, it can be overwhelming at first.

Charlotte was excited so we continued. I whispered to the Tates what word I would be thinking and Charlotte banged out the letters of the thought without hesitation. I asked Phil to think of a word. "Charlotte, what is your dad thinking?" She fumbled on the alpha board. "What's up Charlotte, can you read your dad?" YES "What word is he thinking?" Again she fumbled and wouldn't type anything out. I asked her, "Why won't you read your dad?" She now typed confidently. BECAUSE HE IS MY DAD "OK Charlotte, I understand." She was showing respect for her father. Wow, what a fine person she is. Wait a minute, she reads my mind without worrying about any kind of respect! What's up with that? When I was ready to leave, Charlotte typed out DOING THIS HAS BEEN FUN "Yes, indeed Charlotte, it was a blast. Your parents were pretty impressed with you."

When I returned to school on Monday morning, I was ecstatic. Charlotte had shown her ability to the most important people in her life. I couldn't resist telling Mr. Thomas that Charlotte's parents had witnessed her mind reading ability and were absolutely amazed. He still seemed unfazed and unbelieving. He reminded me of the letter, but he did encourage me to continue to work with Charlotte on generalizing her communication skills with other people. He said that he would talk to any person with whom Charlotte had communicated and that he would document the occurrence if he felt that it was valid. All in all, that wasn't too bad of a conversation.

After Charlotte arrived and put her things away, we went directly into conversation.

"How do you feel today?" PRETTY GOOD

"Do you have a statement?" YES WE SHOWED MY PARENTS SOME PRETTY COOL AND AMAZING THINGS   "Yes we did!"

"Charlotte, Mr. Thomas doesn't want me to work with you on proving that you have autistic talents. He doesn't want me to have you show anyone your mind reading talent. However, he never said that you couldn't use your talents while we work together. Do you understand?" YES

Later that day, I had worked with Sam in the gym. When I returned to the classroom, I asked Charlotte what sign I had seen in the gym. SUCCESS COMES TO THOSE WHO BELIEVE   "That's right Charlotte, do you believe?" YES "I believe too!" I would often repeat that phrase while working with Charlotte for the remainder of the year.

CHAPTER 23

PRIOR TO HIS SECOND VISIT, I looked up Dr. Rogien on the Boise State University Website. I downloaded his biography and read it to Charlotte. She listened as I read the whole page. When he arrived, he cheerfully greeted Charlotte and me. We chatted for a while and I asked Charlotte if she had anything to say. She typed out, TELL HIM TO ADD HUMOR I was a little confused at first but soon understood what she was talking about. At the end of his bio, he had listed five requirements for successful teachers:

1) A variety of teaching models
2) Prevention and intervention plan, and strategies for classroom management
3) A variety of approaches to motivating students
4) Strong personal values including honesty, responsibility, and work ethic
5) Faith in God, themselves, and their students

"You want him to add "humor" to his list of tips for successful teachers?" YES

Dr. Rogien agreed that humor is important. He asked, "Is Dean funny?" YES

Charlotte asked about the manufacturing of an airplane, which was mentioned in the bio. Dr. Rogien talked about working on an airplane and explained about many of the parts he had worked on. Charlotte seemed pretty interested.

Later we continued with a variety of questions......

"What do you think you could do with your abilities that would help and benefit regular people?" MAKE THEM UNDERSTAND HOW AUTISTIC PEOPLE UNDERSTAND THE WORLD

"What made you show me your special abilities last week?" I JUST WANTED TO SHOW YOU

"Do you want to go to college?" YES   "Why?" TO SHOW PEOPLE HOW SMART AUTISTIC PEOPLE ARE

"Do you have any questions about sports?" YES   WHY DO THEY SOMETIMES TAKE GATORADE TO SPORTING EVENTS

"The Gatorade replenishes some of the fluids that the body sweats out."

"Do you have a statement for your parents?" I LOVE YOU BOTH VERY MUCH   THANK YOU FOR UNDERSTANDING MY AUTISM

"What things would you like me to teach you?" STUFF ABOUT HOW THE EARTH STAYS IN ORBIT AROUND THE SUN

"Why do you like it so much when I draw the SpongeBob characters?" YOU DRAW HIM NICELY AND I LIKE TO WATCH PEOPLE DRAW

"Do you have a statement about your special talents?" NO ONE SEES ME DO MY TALENT EXCEPT PEOPLE THAT HAVE A GOOD THOUGHT ABOUT AUTISTIC PEOPLE   "That's fine with me Charlotte, but you'll have to show people outside of the school environment."

The next day....

"How are you feeling today?" TREMENDOUS "Why?" I FEEL TREMENDOUS BECAUSE I AM UNDERSTANDING COMMUNICATION BETTER AND PEOPLE CAN SAY THINGS TO ME   I CAN ANSWER THEM

Charlotte had been communicating with lots of people recently. I reported some of these communication moments to Mr. Thomas in the hopes that he would have tried to corroborate my reports, but to my knowledge, this never happened. After a while, I became disillusioned and stopped telling him anything about Charlotte's communication occurrences. I had been wasting my time. Charlotte had, in fact, communicated with the school principals, the librarian, Clarissa the peer student, her parents and brother, the bus driver and his aide, another teacher at the school, Dr. Rogien, my mother and brother, her former behavior interventionist, and the district's consulting teacher for autism.

I refused to allow Mr. Thomas' ambivalence to dampen my enthusiasm. Fortunately, I could go home each day and report to my family the communication that Charlotte had done that day. It was, and still is, an amazing thing to be part of. Helping a non-communicative person to communicate is something I will value for the rest of my life. I want a paragraph in my obituary to tell about what I was part of with Charlotte and how special our accomplishments were. For the first time in her life, Charlotte could express her thoughts and feelings in an appropriate way. How wonderful for her to do something that the experts thought was impossible.

CHAPTER 24

CHARLOTTE AND I CONTINUED HAVING conversations about autism....

"You wanted to discuss thoughts about people with autism. What thoughts?"

ONLY AUTISTIC PEOPLE UNDERSTAND WHY THEY DO THE THINGS THEY DO

"What do you mean?" WHEN WE FLAP OR SPIN OR DO DIFFERENT THINGS

"Are you trying to say that each person with autism has a way to bring order and to calm their minds?" YES

"Do you have a statement or question?" PEOPLE KEEP CALLING THE HOUSE TO TALK ABOUT MY TALENTS WHAT ARE THEY SAYING ABOUT MY TALENTS I WANT TO KNOW IF MY TALENTS ARE SPECIAL

"I'll ask your folks about the phone calls concerning your talents, but I think your mind reading talent is incredible! Other people with autism might be good with numbers, music, counting, or memorizing things. I've never heard of anyone being able to read minds like you. You are amazing. I looked it up on the internet and only found a couple of references to autistic mind reading. That means that you are a pretty unique human being."

I talked to Angie about the calls. She told me that she had been in contact with a professor who had worked with Charlotte years ago. The professor was excited about the recent communication breakthrough. The professor cautioned that some of the information coming out of Charlotte might be less than accurate. I had, indeed, experienced that when trying to validate some of Charlotte's stories. She had told some whoppers. For example, once when I asked if she had a good weekend, she responded YES   "Do you have a statement?"   YES   I WAS HAPPY TO CELEBRATE EASTER   WE TOOK A TRIP TO THE CABIN IN MCCALL

"Is there still snow on the ground?"   YES

"Did you go to any restaurants?"   YES

"How was the experience?"   I LIKED IT AND BEHAVED WELL THE WAITRESS HAD THESE FUNNY LOOKING PANTS THAT HAD A WALRUS ON IT

This was a story that may have been verifiable, so I checked with Mom. She said that they didn't go anywhere and, in fact, the cabin had been sold. It occurred to me that Charlotte might be describing previous memories.

Another time when she had talked about some women of the night, I was sure that this was a current or recent event in her life, but it turned out to be two years old. Was it possible that in certain instances Charlotte was accessing old memories, or was she just making up stories in order to fulfill her obligation to communicate?

The professor said that many times a person with autism would bond with one person and communicate mainly or exclusively with them. That was a welcomed remark, as it explained why Charlotte would seldom use the alpha board with anyone but me. She also said that the mind reading was not unheard of, but it had never been validated. I relayed this information to Charlotte and she seemed proud of her abilities.

CHAPTER 25

CHARLOTTE'S SOCIAL AND ACADEMIC SKILLS continued to flourish. One day, she went on the mile walk with her classmates. This was a first for her. After the walk, the kids went to the gym and played on little square floor scooters. When they returned, I asked Charlotte, "Why did you go with the group today?" BECAUSE I WANTED TO GO OUTSIDE AND ENJOY THE SUN

"What about the scooters. Did you like them?" YES IT LOOKED LIKE FUN I ABSOLUTELY LOVED THE SCOOTERS

During the next few days.......

"How are you feeling today?" OUTSTANDING

We had been working on pronouncing flashcards and I asked her, "Are there any words you want to learn to pronounce?" YES She then typed out the following, GREAT SAFE LOVE FLOWER BABY GUS KIEFER

The last two are her brothers' names. I wrote each word on an index card and we worked on them daily. I also put the words, MY, NAME, IS, and CHARLOTTE each on a separate card.

"What do you think about the things you are learning in class?" THEY ARE REALLY GOOD

"Do you think we are doing too much work, too little, or about right?" ABOUT RIGHT

"What other things would you like me to teach you about?" HISTORY OF ALASKA   HISTORY OF USA   AZTECS WORLD WAR II

"You are using your words to communicate better and better. Are the railroad tracks coming closer together?" WHAT DO YOU MEAN

I had been using the analogy of a train bringing the words from her brain to her mouth and that her railroad tracks weren't parallel. That was what was interfering with her speech. The train just couldn't get the words to her mouth.

"Is the train bringing the words down from your brain to your mouth a little better?"   YES

Because I was directed to only work on IEP goals, Charlotte's academic activities would have a narrow focus for the remainder of the school year. The IEP goals were: to identify and count coins, pick out the prompted word when two or three words were presented, identify the time on a clock, identify the sequence of the days of the week, answer questions after reading a story, wash her hands before lunch and after using the bathroom, go for walks around school, and identify safety signs.

We would work on the activities for these goals. For the most part, Charlotte did very well. She met most of the goals and I reported these successes in writing each day to Mr. Thomas. But because Charlotte didn't duplicate these efforts with the other aides or for Mr. Thomas, her academic goals were considered to be unattained and unverified.

Fortunately, Charlotte's progress was seen and acknowledged by other professionals. In the middle of the month, the district medical consultant visited our classroom. He had known Charlotte for years, but was unaware of her communication breakthrough. I told him that she could indeed communicate, and Charlotte used the alpha board to answer a variety of YES/NO questions for him. I asked if she had any questions for the doctor. She typed out, ONLY WHAT THE PILLS DO   He explained about her two medications and how they helped her. He asked her, "Do you know my name?"   Charlotte quickly typed it out. The doctor was looking at Charlotte with a nice smile. I asked Charlotte, "What is his face showing?"   HE LOOKS AMAZED. The doctor couldn't believe what he had just witnessed. He left that day with a newfound respect for Charlotte.

More and more, Charlotte was generalizing her communication skills with other people.   One day, when we saw the school resource officer (SRO), he greeted us warmly.   He had always been nice to Charlotte. When I asked if she had a question, she typed out, HOW ARE YOU. He replied, "Fine."   Charlotte's peer mentor, Clarissa, walked up to the three of us and I asked Charlotte if she had anything to say.   SHE IS MY FRIEND

Chapter 26

In May, I wrote a limerick for Charlotte.....

There was a young lady named Char,
Who wanted to drive her own car.
When she drove down the street,
She thought it quite neat.
Until she got stuck in the tar!

After I read it to her she typed out.....THANK YOU FOR WRITING A POEM ABOUT ME

She enjoyed that poem so much that I wrote her another one.

I knew a girl who was far away.
She didn't talk, listen, or play.
Then something clicked inside her head.
Her thirst for knowledge had to be fed.

She typed out her thoughts on an alpha board.
And inside her mind, self esteem soared.
Her behavior improved, she looked forward to school.
Now she could study things that were cool.

Autism is the name of the thing she will beat.
She is trying so hard, it will be a great feat.
Her hope for the future is now really bright.
The sky is the limit, as high as a kite.

She really liked that one too. Angie framed it and put it by Charlotte's bed.

In early June, just before school let out, Charlotte provided a little humor. I was working at getting her to type out responses on the computer. I was being very insistent and persistent. It took a while, but she finally typed out YOU ARE BOSSY. I started cracking up with laughter and told Charlotte she was right. I added, "Sometimes you need me to be bossy to get you to do stuff!" She typed out YES.

The school year ended and the Extended School Year (ESY) began the following week. Many students in Special Education attend ESY in an effort to maintain the skills they had learned. ESY is a six-week program that lasts four hours a day. During this six-week period, Charlotte and I continued to work on her communication skills and her IEP goals. It went by pretty fast and was uneventful.

CHAPTER 27

AT THIS POINT, I NEED to backtrack a little. In the spring of 2005, I looked into going back to college to earn a Special Education Teaching degree. At the age of 49, I had been inspired by Charlotte, my student, to accomplish this task. I felt that if I could succeed with Charlotte, I could succeed with other children as well. I enrolled at Boise State University (home of the 2007 Fiesta Bowl Champions!) and took a special education class during the summer. I received a grade of "A" for the class and I was on my way. At that time, it looked like it would take about four years to complete the program. Shortly after enrolling for fall classes, I received an E-mail from the American Board of Certification for Teacher Excellence (ABCTE). ABCTE is an alternative teacher certification program established through "No Child Left Behind" guidelines. Due to teacher shortages in Idaho, it is one of a handful of states that accepts the ABCTE certification. They let me know that they had added a Special Education certification. The eligibility requirements included a four-year college degree, passing an FBI background check, and passing rigorous testing in Classroom Management, Special Education, and Multiple Academic Subjects. Once registered for the program, all testing must be completed within one year.

Since I already had a four-year college degree, I decided to go this route due to the low cost and short time frame. I gathered and studied lots of recommended materials on the Classroom Management Test and passed my first exam and essay. For the Multiple Academic Subjects test, I borrowed many textbooks from various teachers at the junior high where I had been working. All the teachers were supportive and wished me well. For the most part, I read the materials from cover to cover. US History, World History, Oceanography, Biology, English, Math, Civics, Earth Science, and Economics were some of the books that I actually enjoyed reading more than when I read them some 35 years ago. I studied for about six months for this test and passed it with distinction! I only had one month left to study and take the final Special Education test because of the one-year limit. I read four books and reviewed the notes from the Special Education class that I had taken at BSU. I was a little worried after taking the test, but ended up passing.

The day after taking the last test, my family and I left to go on vacation to the Oregon coast for a week. When we returned, I completed the certified teachers' application for the Boise School District. Unfortunately, there were few positions available, as the school year was to start the following week. It was bad timing on my part, but I knew I would at least have my behavior interventionist position to start off the 2006/2007 school year.

During the summer break, Charlotte's parents had lobbied the special education supervisor for me to join the transition team for the high school Autism Program that Charlotte would be in. However, I had been assigned to Charlotte because of her behavior problems, and because those behaviors were not apparent anymore, the district decided that my services would be better utilized elsewhere. The Tates were very unhappy when they heard that their daughter wouldn't have me to help with her transition to high school. Who would show the new teacher and aides how Charlotte worked and communicated? They would be starting all over again. The Tates said that Charlotte had just experienced the best two years of her public education and now they feared that she was being set up for a downfall. Unfortunately, their concerns would prove to be prophetic.

CHAPTER 28

I WAS ASSIGNED A HIGH school student at the beginning of the school year. I worked with him for the standard eight-week period. I had a fifth grader for my next stint. All along, I was curious about how Charlotte was doing with her new teacher and environment. I found out in early November of 2006.

I was asked to report to Charlotte's new high school to work with her for a day. Phil and Angie were concerned that Charlotte was not progressing or communicating very much in her new classroom. I was tasked with showing the new teacher and aides how I had worked with Charlotte. Hopefully, she would generalize and begin working with them too.

I had conversed with Charlotte only three times in the four months since the Extended School Year, (ESY) had ended. At each of those times, it took a few minutes for Charlotte to get into her typing mode. This day would be no different. Charlotte came in from the bus and looked surprised to see Mr. Dean. She went though her morning routine and put away her backpack, lunch, and coat. She took off her shoes and got her breakfast waffles. I sat by her while she was eating and was excited about communicating with her. She was floundering as she tried to type, but she managed to type out   LEAVE ME ALONE. I inquired, "Do you want to eat?" YES   "Do you want to communicate

159

after you eat?" YES Once again, Charlotte would do things at her pace and on her own schedule.

We did some worksheets which I had gathered from the fifth grade class that I had been working in. Charlotte enjoyed the new assignments and was eager to complete them. She was communicating well after a while. Later that morning, the students went into the main building for break. I was impressed that Charlotte took directions from a petite female aide and was able to use the vending machine. She grounded herself only twice. Once was upon entering and the other upon exiting the building. She also did a few twirls while walking down the hallways.

We returned to the classroom and I demonstrated how Charlotte and I worked on flashcards. Normally, I would say the word and Charlotte would pronounce it as best she could. She would then type it out on a little typing device. On this day however, Charlotte did something different. When I showed her a flashcard of a ball, she immediately started typing BALL on the alpha board that had been positioned on the side of the table. Unlike the way we had usually used the board, it was flat on the table and I wasn't holding it. Later in the day, one of the aides was working with Charlotte on a tiger puzzle. He had been thrilled at how Charlotte and I had communicated using the alpha board and he wanted to try it himself. He held the board up to Charlotte and asked, "What is your favorite animal?" Charlotte quickly typed out TIGER. He was very excited and so was I. In the past, Charlotte had only typed with any consistency when her mother, her brother, or I held the alpha board. It was great to see her generalizing communication with other people.

At lunch, the students and aides marched into the cafeteria. Charlotte had never done that at the junior high and I was thrilled to see her eating with her peers. The rest of the day went well except for one blemish. I wouldn't let Charlotte manicure my cuticles. She liked perfection and wanted to remove any pieces of skin that stuck out. I balled up my hand into a fist so she couldn't get at the fingertips. She was persistent but so was I. In the past, she had peeled off my cuticles like the skin of a banana, which would leave me with painful, open wounds. This time, she grabbed my left arm, squeezed, then switched that squeeze to my right arm in an effort to get to my fingers. Six days later, I still had bruise marks on my forearms. (But I still had my cuticles!)

Soon after that one-day visit, I was asked to work with Charlotte for half a day, each day, from Thanksgiving to Christmas. The supervisor of the high school program said that I was to continue to demonstrate how I worked with Charlotte and to give suggestions and recommendations to the staff. This was just fine with me because the one day I had with Charlotte was not enough.

CHAPTER 29

WHEN I CAME BACK TO work with Charlotte after Thanksgiving, I found that her typing skills had deteriorated quite a bit without consistent usage. She would only type single words and point to YES or NO for answers. On my first day back, it took the whole day for her to get comfortable again using the alpha board to type out a sentence. I also used that first day to get Charlotte reacquainted with my expectations.

On the second day, I wanted Charlotte to have success with activities, so I created a collage. She was visibly excited and quickly wanted to participate in this familiar activity. She demonstrated reading, writing, and speaking. Her writing was very hard to read. Her letters were tiny and overlapped each other. She would improve the size and spacing of her letters over the next couple of days with the implementation of two strategies. First, I got some graphing paper and had Charlotte put one letter in each square. This worked well and allowed her to space her letters better. Second, I wrote sentences describing things that Charlotte had been experiencing at school. She would rewrite each word directly under my writing. This helped her to make her letters and words much more readable.

Charlotte demonstrated her communication abilities with the alpha board in a variety of environments and activities. For example, one morning we returned a tray to the cafeteria. After leaving it on the counter, Charlotte stayed there. I asked her to return to the room, but she maintained her position. The supervisor of the kitchen came over to Charlotte and said, "Hello." Charlotte tried to say something, but it was unintelligible. I offered her the alpha board and she quickly typed out APPLE. I told her, "You can say that word!" She didn't. I helped her by giving her the first syllable. She then loudly said, "Apple!" The lunch lady inquired, "Charlotte, do you want an apple?" Charlotte pointed to YES.

I praised her on our return to the portable. She was proudly holding the apple, but not eating it. That was a little different because generally, when Charlotte got food, she would eat it right away. When we entered the classroom, Charlotte walked right up to the teacher's desk and placed the apple in the middle. I inquired, "Don't you want to eat the apple?" NO "Why did you put in on the desk?" BECAUSE HE IS MY TEACHER   Well, I was just put in my place. I thought I was her teacher. After all, her behavior and academics had flourished under my tutelage over the past two years. I like to think that she meant that he was her teacher now.

Charlotte's communication with the use of the alpha board continued to improve and had almost reached the previous level of six months earlier at the junior high. By the end of my assignment at the high school, Charlotte had typed with the teacher and with two of the special education aides without me facilitating by holding the board. It was great to see her generalizing her communication skills with others.

I prepared a list of recommendations on ways to work with Charlotte. I had tried all of the methods and techniques, and they had provided avenues of success for Charlotte.

1) Give high and low "fives" as praise. She enjoys slapping the hand when it is offered.

2) Wherever you are at school, always have the alpha board with you. It is her voice.

3) Offer her the alpha board often and ask, "Do you have a question or statement?"

4) Don't stop when she objects by making her protest sounds. Work through it.

5) Talk to her often and age appropriately.

6) Use hand over hand for practicing writing letters and numbers.

7) Be persistent and creative.....Think on your feet and try different things. (See number 4)

8) Use the number side of the alpha board to reinforce math equations or monetary values of coins and bills.

9) Be firm and confident when requesting answers.

10) Have high expectations. ASSUME COMPETENCE!!!

11) Have her answer YES/NO questions to get her comfortable using the alpha board with new people.

12) Verify whether or not she's really paying attention by throwing in a question with an obvious answer.

13) Get a peer tutor/mentor from the high school. Charlotte might be nervous at first but will warm up to the student. Facilitate their meeting by using the alpha board so Charlotte has a voice.

14) To keep her interest, be funny, flamboyant, and speak in a louder that normal voice.

15) She will usually answer an open-ended question by pointing to YES. Prompt her to continue her thought.

16) When she makes an error, say, "Aiy, aiy, aiy" (pronounced "eye." This is a queue that she knows and normally will not take offence.

17) If she is fumbling while typing or has hesitated too long, try either of these two things: a) Bop her on the fingers or the back of her typing hand with the alpha board. This helps to redirect her focus. b) Stop, lay the alpha board down, and write down what she had typed before she started to fumble. This allows her time to regroup and refocus. She'll want to read what you have written, and will usually continue from that point.

18) If she hovers over the letter R when beginning a sentence, she usually wants ARE. Tell her to "Get the right letter." She'll go to A, then RE.

I left these recommendations with the teacher and staff in the hopes that they would enjoy some success as I had while working with Charlotte. Due to the reprimand I had received the previous year, I neglected to tell them about Charlotte's amazing mind reading ability or her other possible savant talents. If Charlotte wanted to let them know about these skills, she would show them at her own pace.

CHAPTER 30

IN JANUARY, I WAS REASSIGNED to an elementary school where I worked in a special education classroom for kids with various types and degrees of autism. I often wondered how Charlotte was doing. Evidently, Charlotte had been behaving well at school. She had only pounded on the hood of a car once while returning from the main building. In early April, however, Charlotte had a behavior escalation while working on the computer. Angie and Phil were called because of the emergency. When they arrived, they witnessed people holding Charlotte down and a policeman trying to apply handcuffs. Fortunately, Charlotte calmed quickly when she saw her parents. The supervisor of the Autism Program contacted my supervisor, who, in turn, contacted my current classroom teacher. Once again, I was to report to the high school for the following week.

I was tasked with helping to determine what level of academic instruction Charlotte was capable of doing. The Tates were insisting on having some kind of curriculum for Charlotte. They were tired of the same old, low grade-level worksheets that Charlotte had been bringing home throughout the year. Maybe this low expectation of Charlotte's abilities had contributed to her behavior. She was bored in school and was allowed to take naps daily. Charlotte's high school teacher asked me to focus on reading, math, and history. He also wanted me to continue demonstrating communication with Charlotte by using the alpha board.

I told the supervisor and the teacher that my initial focus would be on increasing communication with the alpha board. She would need this skill if she was going to be successful in showing her capabilities in the other subject areas.

At the beginning of class on my first day back, Charlotte was enjoying her waffle breakfast, which she had most days. I didn't press her to communicate during breakfast because it had annoyed her in the past. However, even when she did finish, she was reluctant to type at all.

We took our morning walk to the library. I asked her what kind of book she wanted. She typed out AUTISM. I asked the librarian about the topic and she brought us to a section with two books on autism. Charlotte selected the book about a woman with autism. The librarian checked it out to Charlotte. I asked her if she had something to say to the librarian. Charlotte typed out THANKS. The librarian then introduced herself and asked Charlotte if she had anything to say. She typed out I AM CHARLOTTE

On the way back to the classroom, I asked Charlotte why she wasn't communicating much with me. She didn't answer. This led me to inquire, "Are you mad at me?" YES "Why?" BECAUSE YOU LEFT ME ALL ALONE AT SCHOOL   That response certainly explained why she wasn't communicating well with me. She was under the impression that I chose not to be her teacher.

I explained that the supervisors told me where I would work. It wasn't my decision to not be her teacher this year. "Are you still mad at me?" YES "Charlotte, I like working with you. It wasn't my fault. My boss tells me where I have to work and I have to go there. Do you understand?" YES "Are you still mad at me?"   NO She began typing much better with me after we cleared the air.

Charlotte did some math in front of the classroom teacher. He was surprised that she could do addition and multiplication and communicate her answers by using the alpha board. She correctly answered 19 out of 20 questions, then corrected the one she missed.

For history that day, I had a textbook and read a four-page passage on the ancient Indians of North America. Charlotte listened intently. I had written down eight vocabulary words on the left side of the page and their definitions in random order on the right side. Charlotte was to draw a line from the vocabulary word to its correct definition. She understood and began. She got five correct and she corrected the remaining three on the first "redo."

That day, Charlotte wanted to eat her lunch early. She grabbed her meal and stood by the microwave. There was another aide present and we both played dumb. "What do you want?" The aide offered her the alpha board and Charlotte typed out I WANT LUNCH Once again, she was generalizing her communication with someone other than myself.

After lunch, I brought out the alpha board and asked, "Do you have any questions or statements?" DEAN REALLY YOU CAN STILL MAKE ME LAUGH   YOU ARE THE ONLY ONE WHO CAN MAKE ME LAUGH "Thanks Tate, I like making you laugh!"

On Tuesday, Charlotte pronounced 20 flashcards, then typed each one on her portable typing device. She clearly pronounced flower, bird, apple, and popcorn with little or no prompting. For the other words, I said the first syllable before she followed with the whole word. Most of her words were understandable. She seemed excited about talking.

But her attitude seemed to change when it came to typing for me. She started plenty of sentences, but left them incomplete. Later that day, she did the same when communicating with the PE teacher and another aide.

I was concerned about her lack of enthusiasm for communicating with the alpha board. I grabbed the board and began asking YES/NO questions. I would go back to the basics to warm her up to the idea of communicating.

"Are you still mad at me?" YES "Why?" No response. "Are you mad because I am only here for a short while?" YES I threw in a verifiable question. "Do you want me to jump off the roof?" NO "Are you going to talk to me tomorrow?" NO "Are you being stubborn?" YES Again I asked a verifiable question. "Can you walk through a wall?" NO "Miss stubborn, do you want me to come back tomorrow?" YES

Overall, it was a disappointing day for me. She had never shut me out like that. She did demonstrate that she had the same feelings as a regular person. She thought I had abandoned her at school and she had no qualms about letting me know. Maybe that was why she had given the classroom teacher the apple. She was letting me know that she was unhappy with me, and tried to make me upset by showing me that she considered the classroom teacher her teacher and not me.

Wednesday started out with a poor showing in academics. After I read a "Read Naturally" story, I asked her four questions with multiple choice answers. She correctly circled the answer for the first question, then proceeded to circle all four choices for each of the next three questions.

Our history session provided similar results. I read a new passage about ancient Indians. Charlotte listened well and pointed to YES when I asked if she understood what I had just read. I gave her a glue stick and slips of paper with the answers to the questions. She only glued one answer to the correct question. She needed a lot of prompting and explaining to get the other four correct.

When I tried communicating with her later that day, I decided to appeal to her sense of humanity. "Humans communicate with each other. Are you human?" YES "Smart people communicate with each other. Are you smart?" YES "Are you still mad at me?" YES "Because I am only here for a short time?" YES "Do you want me to leave?" NO "Do you want me to stay?" YES I could see that I had my work cut out for me.

After lunch, she wanted another student's Cheetos, which were stored in one of the cabinets. She just kept whining. I told her, "This is a no whine zone. Get the alpha board. I don't understand whining." I thought it was necessary that she utilize the board even though it was obvious what she wanted. The alpha board was on the counter and she grabbed it. She typed out CHEETOS to another aide that had ventured into the kitchen. He directed her to the student who owned the Cheetos and asked if Charlotte could have some. The student agreed to give some to her.

At the end of the day, I asked her again, "Tell me why you are mad at me." BECAUSE YOU ARE LEAVING TOO SOON I told her that I was sorry that I would only be there one week, but we should take advantage of the final two days and have some fun.

It seems as though I got through to Charlotte. On Thursday, she had a great turn-a-round with communication. She was typing words, sentences, and lots of appropriate YES/NO responses.

I gave her some simple algebra equations for math. She wasn't interested, so I switched to number sequences. I wrote nine problems, each with three consecutive numbers and she was to tell me what number came next. She nailed all of them perfectly and on the first try.

Our special education class was invited to the cafeteria to play some games with students from a health class. I sat down with the two girls assigned to play with Charlotte. Charlotte was standing across the room from us near a cafeteria kitchen counter. Charlotte's teacher and I kept prompting her to join the group at the table, but Charlotte wasn't enthralled with that prospect. After five minutes, she finally came over and sat down. I asked the two girls to introduce themselves. Lucy and Amanda said their names and I gave Charlotte the alpha board. She immediately typed out CHARLOTTE. We played a game that required the sequencing of chronological events in a story. Charlotte showed that she understood the order of events. I commented to her, "This is a game where you have to put things in order of occurrence. What is that called?" SEQUENCING The two girls were impressed and one stated that she couldn't even spell that word.

When a story came up featuring a boy diving off a board, I asked Charlotte if she knew why the boy went into the water rather than continuing up into the air. I further clarified my question. "What makes things fall to earth?" It took a little while, but she finally typed out GRAVITY. "Did you have fun playing the game with these two girls?" YES Charlotte was comfortable with the girls the whole time and that was nice to see. She definitely represented herself well with her general education peers.

After that positive experience, I discussed with Charlotte's teacher the benefits of having student peers for Charlotte. I had endorsed that at the junior high and included it in my previous recommendations. He said it was too late in the year, but maybe he could get something going next year. I had high hopes that he would follow through.

Charlotte's dad came in that afternoon and excitedly told me that Charlotte had typed for him the previous night. Phil was very happy with that. At home, Charlotte had only been typing regularly with her mom. Phil brought in a video camera and taped Charlotte communicating by using the alpha board. She answered lots of questions and completed number sequences. She also typed out the names of the two girls that had played the game with her earlier in the day.

On our final day together, Charlotte and I did a fun activity with word association using flashcards. "Charlotte, what comes to mind when you see........"

Flashcard	Charlotte typed
baby	CRY
ball	ROLL
bag	FOOD
blue	SKIES
bed	SLEEP
bear	WINNIE (the Pooh)
beehive	RUN (I had a chuckle with that reply)
butterfly	RED
bus	YELLOW
barn	HAY
amigo	FRIEND

Overall, the week was a success. The staff got to see how Charlotte could work on various academic subjects using different formats. She communicated with two aides and with the teacher using the alpha board. They were holding the board, not me. This was important as it showed that she was generalizing her skills with others. She also typed responses to questions from other high school staff and students.

The teacher now had an idea about Charlotte's abilities in history, reading, and math. He knew that he would have to collect appropriate curriculum materials for the rest of the year. Although it was late in the school year, I felt that things might finally be on the right track for Charlotte to progress and be successful at school.

CHAPTER 31

THAT SUMMER, I HAD BEEN hired as a special education teacher for the Extended School Year (ESY) program at an elementary school. Angie contacted me and asked if I would work with Charlotte during the summer. She would bring her to my class twice a week after school. She told me that the district had hired a new teacher for the high school Autism Program who was coincidentally, working at my summer school. This was a perfect opportunity for the new teacher to see how Charlotte worked and communicated. I hoped that she would be able to observe and work with Charlotte that summer and I received approval from the principal for that to happen..

On our first after-school session, Charlotte asked, ARE YOU DEAN GOING TO RETURN TO BE MY TEACHER   Angie and I both choked up. I managed to reply, "No Charlotte, we will be working together for a few hours a week during the summer. You will be able to meet and get to know your new teacher." She looked sad and disappointed, but she was a trooper and continued to work.

Later that summer, the new teacher watched Charlotte and I communicating with the use of the alpha board. She then tried it herself. At first, Charlotte was a bit apprehensive. I told the teacher to ask an obvious question like, "What is the name of your high school?" She did, and Charlotte typed it out for her. I was happy to see that the ice had been broken. The teacher would continue to work with Charlotte during the summer and had some success in facilitating communication.

About two weeks into the ESY program, I received a job offer from a neighboring school district to be a special education teacher at a high school. I had hoped that my district would have hired me, but that was just not happening. This was disappointing to me, as I thought I had served the district well and deserved a shot at a teaching position. I had definitely gone the extra mile and was successful in my efforts with Charlotte. Maybe my earlier exuberance in proclaiming that Charlotte could communicate and that she had special talents was coming back to haunt me. Maybe my decision to develop a relationship with Charlotte's parents had something to do with the district's position. Who knows? Maybe the right job for me just was not available in that district. I do know that in retrospect, I would do it all again and not change a thing. I had been an unequivocal advocate for my student, and had been proven right about her communication and other incredible skills and talents. I enthusiastically accepted the job offer with the new district, but with me leaving Charlotte's district, it became even more imperative for the Tates to document Charlotte's progress in working and communicating. Her district could no longer rely on Mr. Dean to demonstrate successful methods and strategies to use with Charlotte. The Tates videotaped Charlotte and me working together to show that she could communicate and how I successfully got her to do academics.

Charlotte, Angie, and I met occasionally for some tutoring sessions after I left the district. We worked on a variety of subjects and Charlotte was always engaged with the efforts. We usually worked for an hour, but sometimes Charlotte would want to bug out early. Many times, Charlotte would hold the alpha board herself and type out her message. This was wonderful to see.

CHAPTER 32

WHAT WILL THE FUTURE HOLD for Charlotte? Will she generalize her communication skills with other people to the level that she had with me? I can only hope that she will. I do believe she has the ability to do that, but I fear that her desire is questionable. She does things at her own pace according to her own desires and may choose not to communicate, especially with strangers. Deep down, Charlotte is a shy person. I wish I had another two years with her in a school setting. I am confident that if I had that amount of time with her, she would be able to increase her communication with other people and maybe even initiate more verbal language. I encouraged her to communicate with a variety of people in order to get her confidence level up and to give her practice in using the alpha board. I fear that she will have only a small circle of familiar people with whom she will communicate. But even if she only communicates with her family in the future, it will still be a major accomplishment. Many people with autism never learn to communicate, and to start at the age of 16 is practically unheard of.

What could Charlotte do with her mind-reading ability? It would be great if she could make a living by using that talent. There must be hundreds of opportunities or careers where she could utilize her ability. Could Charlotte work in law enforcement in some capacity? Would she be able to read a suspect's mind and determine if he had an accomplice? Would she know where the suspect was hiding evidence or much worse, a kidnapped victim? Could she sit in on an FBI or CIA interrogation of a terrorist and know where a bomb was hidden? Who knows what she would be capable of doing if her talent could be harnessed and honed?

Charlotte had indicated that she could read the minds of people with autism. Could she work as a facilitator between a person with autism and their parents or instructors? She could read their thoughts and let others know what is going on in their heads. She could give hope to parents by letting them know that their child's mind was intact, but governed by the autistic disability. Charlotte was always very caring with physically disabled students in her PE class. I think she could use this caring attitude in some way while working with people with autism.

Could Charlotte use her talent to read the minds of comatose patients? This could help families know the thoughts and desires of the patient and also give them hope that their loved ones were still "in there somewhere." Paralyzed people who can't talk might also benefit from being able to communicate through Charlotte. There are lots of possibilities for Charlotte to pursue. If she were able to utilize her mind-reading ability successfully, there could be a plethora of employment opportunities. This would enable her to become economically self-sufficient.

Regardless of what she could do with her talent, safeguards would need to be in place to protect her. She has led a sheltered life, and exposure to the ugliness of what humans are capable of might be more than she needs to experience. Her parents would be instrumental in sorting through the details of any endeavor.

It will always be special to me to know that I made a difference in another human being's life. She may never stand in front of her classmates at graduation and say a few words like she did in my hopes and dreams. Those dreams, however, provided me with the patience, hope, and energy that it took for me to fulfill my obligations and responsibilities as her teacher. It was a pleasure and an honor to work with Charlotte. She was indeed reachable and teachable.

Thank you Charlotte for inspiring me to pursue a teaching career and become a teacher. THANK YOU DEAN FOR TEACHING ME AND HELPING ME UNDERSTAND COMMUNICATION

The End????

AFTERTHOUGHTS

I WANT TO THANK DR. Rogien for giving me the impetus to consider writing the story in the first place. I doubt if the story would have been told without his gentle "push" for me to write it. A special thanks goes to Marcia, my editor. She worked many hours on smoothing out the rough spots. Her efforts were invaluable and her enthusiasm was appreciated. To Charlotte and her family for allowing me to write her incredible story, I thank you. And finally, thank you to my family who put up with me throughout the writing, typing, and editing phases of the book. Also, some of the names of people mentioned in the story have been changed.

A SPECIAL NOTE FROM
CHARLOTTE'S MOTHER, ANGIE TATE

IT IS NOT THE END, *but a story must begin somewhere and Charlotte's communication by typing started with a wonderful teacher, Dean LeBreton. How do you thank someone for that?*

Charlotte has been exposed to numerous methodologies designed for students with autism. She attended an early intervention program for three years, run by Dr. Mike Day, mastering the program with the exception of receptive language. As a preschooler, she would match hundreds of words to their corresponding pictures or objects. After preschool, she was introduced to The Picture Exchange Communication System (PECS). She had a couple hundred pictures with words in her PECS book. These structured programs gave Charlotte the opportunity to learn to read and acquire a vocabulary.

Charlotte was taught throughout her early years using Applied Behavior Analysis, PECS, The Miller Method, Gentle Teaching, and The Reading and Writing Program to name a few. She wore Arlen Lenses for a time, tried secretin injections, mega vitamins, a diet without wheat and dairy, probiotics, and had the help of many talented Occupational, Physical, and Speech therapists and consultants. The Rapid Prompting Method gave Charlotte a voice. Dean believed in Charlotte, worked with her, and wouldn't give up on her.

Charlotte is currently attending her senior year of high school. She has been to camp at HALO (Helping Autism through Learning and Outreach) two additional times since the first camp with Dean. Her current high school special education teacher has completed Level 1 training at HALO. Now that Charlotte can type independently, with one hand holding her letter board and one hand typing, her communication ability is believed in a school environment.

Charlotte plans to attend college in the future and tells us she would like to live with roommates to help her with the daily challenges of autism.

Under Charlotte's picture in the high school yearbook she typed a message to her peers:

"Even though I have autism I am smart and very happy. Objectively, autism is only part of who I am. You can have autism and still be very able to study. To happy lives." Charlotte (Lottie) Tate.

Printed in the United States
148797LV00004B/2/P